Buddha in the Looking Glass

Further Zen Ramblings from the Internet

Scott Shaw

Buddha Rose Publications

Buddha in the Looking Glass
Further Zen Ramblings from the Internet
Copyright © 2017 by Scott Shaw
www.scottshaw.com
All Rights Reserved

No Part of this book may be reproduced in any manner without the expressed written permission of the author or the publishing company.

Cover photographs by Scott Shaw
Copyright © 2017 All Rights Reserved

Rear cover photographs of Scott Shaw by Hae Won Shin
Copyright © 2017 All Rights Reserved

First Edition 2017

ISBN 10: 1-877792-98-5
ISBN 13: 978-1-877792-98-4

Library of Congress: 2017958999

Printed in the United States of America

10 9 8 7 6 5 4 3 2 1

Buddha in the Looking Glass

Introduction

Here it is, *The Scott Shaw Zen Blog 9.0,* originally presented on the World Wide Web. All of the writings presented in this book were written between July and October 2017.

As was the case with the previously published volumes based upon *The Scott Shaw Zen Blog;* entitled: *Scribbles on the Restroom Wall*, *The Chronicles: Zen Ramblings from the Internet*, *Words in the Wind, Zen Mind Life Thoughts, The Zen of Life, Lies, and Aberrant Reality, Apostrophe Zen, The Abstract Arsenal of Zen, Zen and Again: The Metaphysical Philosophy of Psychology, and Tempest in a Teapot and the Den of Zen* this volume is presented exactly as it was viewed on scottshaw.com with no rewriting, punctuation, or typo corrections. From this, we hope you will receive the original reading experience.

This volume of internet ramblings is presented with the date and time listed as to when each blog was originally posted. Also, the blogs in this volume are presented from last to first. With this, we hope to present a transcendence back through time as opposed to an evolving evolution. In addition, we left out the traditional *Table of Contents* in an attempt to leave this volume with a much more free-flowing reading experience.

Okay, there's the information and the definitions. Read on… We hope you enjoy it. And, be sure to stayed tuned for the ongoing *Scott Shaw Zen Blog* @ scottshaw.com.

*   *   *
24/Oct/2017 03:34 PM

If you want it for free, that means you are giving the person who created it nothing.

But, if they didn't create it, you couldn't want it.

If you want it, you owe the person who created it something.

Why are you unwilling to pay your debt?

*   *   *

24/Oct/2017 07:51 AM

Somebody is saying something negative. Whether it is right or wrong, truth or fiction is irrelevant. If you are about the betterment of everyone, it is your job to intercede and say something positive. End the trend.

The Helping Hand
23/Oct/2017 07:48 AM

I frequently ask people the question, *"What are you going to do today that will help somebody other than yourself?"* Right now, answer that question.

For most, they do not have an answer to that question because they do not think of other people, they only think about themselves. For others, the ones that actually pretend to care, they may attempt to come up with a suitable sounding answer. But, is that actually a real answer? Have they actually preplanned to do something for someone else?

As we pass through life, the <u>something</u> in most everyone's life is themselves. That something is based upon what they want and how they want to feel. If someone else enters into that calculation, equaling something that they want or someone who makes them feel the way they want to feel, then that person is the person they may considering doing something for. But, is that, *"Doing,"* in its purest sense? Or, again, is that just <u>doing</u> for yourself? I believe the answer to that question is clear.

The other factor in this equation is that people are quick to dismiss, *"That person doesn't need my help or there is nothing that I could do to help them."* Dismissal is easy. But, dismissal is just as the definition of the term implies, it is you not even caring enough to care or you not trying hard enough to try. Dismissal is easy. Trying takes caring focus. It takes effort.

So, again, we come to the place where the question must be asked, *"What are you going to do today that will help somebody other than yourself?"* Can you shake your mind out of its commonality of self-thought and actually care enough to do?

As we all can view our own lives as a basis for understanding, I frequently pose this question to myself. I do this to:

1. Shake my mind free of self-absorptions.
2. To make sure that I am caring enough to care at all junctures of my life.

So, right now, ask yourself, *"What can you do that will make someone's life just a little bit better and are you willing to do it?"*

As we can look to our own life as a basis for understanding, every now and then I take stock of what people have done for me. When someone does something nice for me and it comes my direction out of the unexpected nowhere I always extend my sincerest appreciation. Other times, I question why does no one cares enough to care—to say or do something nice? It is at those times when I (when we) should study our own pathway and first of all remove the self-motivated desires which equal obstacles. For if we open our eyes we may see that if all we are desiring is the only thing that we will believe is a, *"Doing,"* than we may miss the fact that there are people out there caring about us, and doing things for us, in their own small way.

At the end of our days, our life will not be measured by what we did for ourselves. It will be judged by what we did for others. So, *"What are you going to do today that will help somebody other than yourself?"* Right now, answer that question. Right now, go and do something for someone you know, someone you don't know, someone you like, or someone you hate. Caring and doing good is always the best thing to do!

The Casting Couch
21/Oct/2017 07:15 AM

Recently, the experiences of actresses and actors experiencing sexual exploitation at the hands of powerful industry professional has been at the forefront of the news. This is a sign of the times and it demonstrates the changing and refining mindset of people and what they are willing and/or not willing to take. And, this is a good thing. But, it is essential to note, that this has been going on forever. Is there anyone out there who doesn't know what the term, *"The casting couch,"* implies. Meaning, this is such a prevalent form of industry interaction that it actually has been given a name.

Recently, TMZ found some older, major player in the industry coming out of a restaurant. All he had to say was that this had been going on for a hundred years. It was known and it was accepted.

For all of those A-List players out there claiming that they knew nothing about it, I call bullshit. They are lying! Even Tarantino, in his recently interview on the subject, dodged his responsibility in this issue. At least he said, *"Anything I say will only sound like an excuse."* But, think about this, if you watch his films, either the character he plays or another primary character sexually assaults a woman (or man). I have always found this very offensive. Though he is undoubtedly a great auteur, this behavior is just wrong and it should never be glorified in a movie! Plus, virtually all of his films were produced by Harvey Weinstein (the man at the center of this controversy). In fact, when this crisis broke, one of the news networks rightly stated that there has virtually been no Academy Awards Ceremony, in the past twenty years, where someone has not thanked Harvey Weinstein. He is responsible for making some incredible movies. In fact, a couple of his accusers thanked him at these ceremonies. What does this tell us?

Personally, in the independent industry, I have known so many actresses who would tell me things like, *"I had to fuck him to be in his movie."* Or, *"I don't want to be in any more of his films because I would have to fuck him again."* And, these are not major A-Films like Weinstein produces. These are crappy low-budget pieces created by ugly, fat, old men. Even my Zen Filmmaking buddy Don Jackson was like this. If an actress wasn't forthcoming with sexual favors he would take them on what he called, *"The Don walk."* I always found that so disgusting. I felt so sorry for the actresses. But, at least, he was not forceful, they could say, *"No."*

On the other side of the of the issue, there has been times when an actress, when I was casting a movie, has done things like reach her hand across the desk, take a hold of my hand, and say, *"I will do anything to be in this movie."* Though tempting, as these were beautiful women, that is just not who I am. There was only one time when I walked down the road of romance with an actress in one of my films but that was based on mutual attraction. But, unfortunately, due to various circumstances, as is the case with many new relationships, that one never had the opportunity to mature.

#metoo. Women are not the only ones who are sexual exploited in the industry. As has been well documented, men too encountered sexually inappropriate behavior. There are two instances, in my career, that come to mind. The first was with a high-powered casting agent. She was a bit older women, who, in her youth, was probably very attractive. After I had gone to the casting session, I was outside getting on my Harley. She ran out to talk to me. What occurred is that she invited me to go to a coffee house with her. I politely declined as I could see what was on her mind. Her facial expression immediately changed. *"You know, I'm your only chance or you're never going to work in this industry,"* was her statement. I smiled and rode off. But, she was right. My budding career in the A-market pretty much ended at that moment. Certain people, in Hollywood, have massive power.

The second time occurred with a manager; a woman, who took me on as her client. Again, she was somewhat older and had recently broken up from a relationship with a younger actor who she had guided into starring roles in a few A-films. I quickly came to understand what she was expecting from me but me, being nice and naïve, I thought I could sidestep this industry requirement. At one point, she invited me to watch a Hong Kong Kung Fu movie with her, which were beginning to become cult-mainstream at that point in history. Me, I showed up with my girlfriend. Well… That ended that. No more manager.

The fact is, most people in Hollywood are willing to do whatever it would take to enter into a position where they would be given the chance to star in an A-film. That is why this has gone on for so long. #metoo. Believe me, if one of those women would have said if you have sex with me I will give you a starring role in a major A-film, I would have happily done it. But, the sad thing is, Hollywood is all about the illusion and the power-play. And, like I have long said, *"The number one rule of filmmaker is that everybody lies."* So, you can't trust anybody!

Mostly, the people that have been in the news, on this subject, are the major female A-players who have been blessed enough to climb to the top. Were they in Weinstein productions? Yes, several of them. What they had to do to climb to the top of the ladder, I guess we will never truly know. But, they are there. We can only speculate if it was worth it.

The other people out there talking are those who did not reach any level of known success. Thus, they are trying to grab a moment of PR. God bless 'em! But, as history has shown us, there is always the powerful at the top and those who desire to be there. From this, some exert their power, while others are willing to do whatever it takes to gain that power. So, what does this teach us? What it teaches us is that the majority of people base their life upon desire. If you do base your life upon desire, then you are going to encounter those people who also base their life upon desire. From this, comes desire attempting to overpower other desire. So, from a Zen perspective we can conclude, remove desire from the equation and you are free.

      Are you free enough to be free? Or, do you desire? If you desire, then the result(s) of your life, and those you will encounter, are obvious. Your life, your choice. Desire, and there is a price to pay. No desire, you are free.

*   *   *
20/Oct/2017 05:15 PM

If a person tells you that what you are doing is hurting them or is causing their life damage and you do not stop the action and apologize, that means that you are a person who does not care about the feelings of others. What do you think will be the end result of your life?

* * *

20/Oct/2017 05:12 PM

The achievers work towards obtaining their desired achievement. Those who do not achieve talk about those who have achieved. Which do you believe is better?

* * *
20/Oct/2017 03:20 PM

If you are not honorable enough to honor another person's wishes that means you have no honor.

* * *

20/Oct/2017 03:19 PM

It's easy to say what's wrong with someone else. How willing are you to tell the world what's wrong with you?

Paying for Your Future Sins
19/Oct/2017 01:17 PM

What you have done has set a continuity of karma into motion. What you have done has set you up for the next chain of events that you will encounter in your life.

If what you have done has hurt someone, that hurt will continue until you undo that damage.

How much time do you spend thinking about the damage you have caused to someone's life? How much time do you spend making mental excuses for what you have done and why you did it? And, how much time do you spend attempting to correct it?

This is where people completely misunderstand the concept of karma and why they question the powers-that-be when negative events befalls them.

You cannot undo any negative karma you have unleashed onto one person by doing something nice or good for someone else.

If you have hurt someone, you have hurt someone. Until you have repaired the damage with that one specific person; you, your karma, and your destiny will be forever defined by the hurt you have unleashed.

As what you have done defines what will come to you in the future, your present moment can also be impacted by what you will do in the future. Meaning, what you do to one person, and the way you react to what you have done, defines how you will behave in the future. People rarely change. People rarely change in the way that they interact with other people and/or care about other people. If you do not care about the damage that you brought to one person's life today, the fact is, you will probably not care about the damage that you bring to another person's life in the future. Thus, your destiny is cast in stone.

So, the next time you encounter something negative in your life—the next time you question, *"Why me?"* Look to yourself. Look to the damage you have done in the past. Look to the damage you will do in the future. Then, the answer to your question of, *"Why me,"* will become obvious.

* * *

19/Oct/2017 01:17 PM

Why haven't you?

It's a very simple question.

I Didn't Even Think About That
19/Oct/2017 07:38 AM

Each of us, as we pass through life, will encounter a moment when we realize that we made the wrong decision; we went left when we should have gone right. But, the general truth of this realization comes from the fact that, *"I didn't even think about that."* We made our choice based upon what we knew/what we believed was available to us at the time. We made that decision upon what opportunities we believed that we had. But then, it was only later, that we come to understand that we could have lived a better/different life if only we had made a different decision.

The truth of the choices that we make are based upon many factors. Mostly, they are predicated upon what is in front of us—what is on our plate if you will. For it is there, right in front of our eyes, that we believe we see the obvious. But, the obvious is generally full of illusions. And, from this, many a life goes wrong.

The choices that we make, based upon the obvious, are commonly shared by everyone who exists in a specific culture at a precise point in history. They can be the school we choose to attend, the major we choose for our studies, the job we take, how we spend our money, the car or motorcycle we buy, what we eat, drink, and/or if we choose to smoke or ingest mind altering substances, onto the person we choose to be in a relationship with. Whereas some of these choices may turn out to be a benefit to our life; a choice well-made—they each may also totally alter our existence in a negative manner, as well. Yet, we made a choice. We choose to let those things into our lives. Now what?

Once the realization hits you that you made the wrong choice, and it will come to everyone at some point in their life, you are left with the, *"What should I do next?"* In some cases, the choices you've made can be altered. In other cases, they cannot. The younger you have this realization, the easier it is to change your course. But, the truth of choice is that you will never be the same once that choice has been made. Your life will forever be defined by that choice.

Certainly, the personal choices that we make in association with what we do with our bodies, has long term effects. Effects that may not be felt until many years later. This is the same with what we believe are the right things to do with people—for it is with/from people where so much of what we have to justify, (the what we did and why), comes from.

Relationships are forever one of the main factors that comes to define a person's life, either in a positive or negative way. People meet someone. They choose to be them. But, think about how many of those relationship go wrong. Why do so many relationships go wrong? Because the people who enter into these relationship enter into them based upon an undefined/not clearly refined mental perspective, believing that person is the only choice that is available.

So okay… We've all made mistakes, we've all made a choice, we have all realized that we probably should have done something else, at some point in our life. From this, some people lament endlessly. They drive themselves deeply into anxiety and depression, constantly thinking about the school they should have gone to, the subject they should have studied, the job they should not have taken, the drink they should not have drank, the cigarette they should not have smoked, the money they should not have spent, the person they should never have been with.

Yes, you can lament. Yes, you can hate your life. Yes, you can beat yourself up for the choices that you made and the things that you did based upon the choices that you made or you can do something else—do something different.

Certainly, the older you get the harder it is to go back to school. The older you get the harder it is to change careers. The older you get finding a relationship with that young, attractive person, that you wish you would have met when you were twenty becomes nearly impossible. But, you can change the, *"Who you are."* You can change the way you behave based upon the choices you made: one, ten, or thirty years ago. You can become a new you in the space where you find yourself, based upon the choices you made however many years ago.

And, this is what people don't do. This is why people never evolve. This is why people never change. This is why people never achieve any of the anything that they wish they could have achieved.

Yes, you made a choice which set a course of direction for your life. But, even if you can't change that choice, you can change who you are on the inside. You can refine that person you became, due to the choices that you made. You can set your life on a course, defined by where you find yourself in life, that will allow you to be the most perfect example of what you hoped you would be. But, you have to make the choice to do it.

* * *
 18/Oct/2017 02:03 PM

People are flawed. Thus, no matter what rank, title, or distinction they claim you should never listen to them for, at best, they are only discussing life from their own perspective.

Don't Do Me Any Favors
18/Oct/2017 10:19 AM

It is rather interesting, in this modern day and age, one of the primary key words of internet piracy is, *"Fair Use."* Basically, what Fair Use means is, *"Let me make money or get famous off of what you created while not paying you, the creator, a red cent."*

I often go back to this subject in this blog, my writings, and my lectures, because of being on the creative end of this equitation—the one who actually creates stuff, I am the one who personally experiences the negative repercussions of so-called Fair Use. Sure, you can sue the people who do this, and I have done this and won, but a lot of what takes place is going on off-shore or by some disposable LLC or someone who, even when you win the lawsuit, there is nothing that you are going to gain because they have no money. So, the creator is the one who is left to deal with the negative repercussions of this larceny and their bank account is lessoned by what someone else chose to do with their creation. Do you not understand the problem in all of this?

Recently, I found that this guy had uploaded a bunch of my music to this website. Of course, the website makes money from every download. They do this while claiming Fair Use. Yet me, the creator, makes nothing. I contacted the guy as it linked to the member who uploaded the music and ask him why did he do it. He said he really liked my music and wanted to help me with publicity. I told him, *"Thanks. But, don't do me any favors."*

Now, I have also encountered companies that are very honest. When they have been broadcasting my movies and I altered them to the fact that I own all Rights, Title, and Interest to the film they either stopped allowing it to be downloaded or set up a deal and paid me. But, that is rare.

Think about this, when you are on the internet and you want to watch or listen to something, maybe you even really love the project or the creator, (as the aforementioned guy did with my music), do you even consider if they, the creator, is getting paid while you are getting their creations for free? And, do you care?

If you like something to even if you love to hate it, shouldn't the person who created it be the only one getting paid for its dissemination? …Not someone who had nothing to do with anything?

Living a good life is based upon morality. Morality is defined by what you do to others.

What do you do to others? And, are you strong enough to not do it and not support the people who are doing it, if what they are doing is taking something away from the person who is responsible for a somethings creation?

Like I always say, all life beings with you. What are you going to do? Are you going to support the creator(s) or are simply going to take their creations for free?

Perceptions of Me
17/Oct/2017 03:39 PM

I forever find it curious (and interesting) the way people perceive me. I mean, how many of you who read this blog actually know me? How many of you have actually met me? How many of you have contacted me and/or tried to meet me? Yet, all of you people out there who have never met me, you have a perceived notion about me. Some of you maybe like what I write; maybe you like some of movies, music, or photographs. Maybe it's just the opposite, you hate me for some undisclosed reason. But, do you ever ask yourself, *"Why do I perceive Scott Shaw the way that I do? What am I basing my opinion upon?"*

I had an interesting experience that set me to thinking about this yesterday… A young filmmaker, going to film school at USC, contacted me via one of the industry casting websites, inquiring if I would be interested in being in her film. Now, I really don't know what she was expecting? Did she want me to audition, did she want me to go to rehearsals—I don't know? But, I told her the same basic thing that I pretty much tell everyone, (and any of you indie filmmakers who have asked me to be in your no-budget film can attest to this fact), I told her, *"Thanks, but the only bad movies I'm in are my own..."* But, as she was a USC student—meaning she was coming at the film game from a slightly different, more refined, perspective than the person out there trying to make an indie movie that will launch their career and make them a buck… So, I said, if she wanted to send me the script I would check it out and see if I believed that I could do the character justice. But, I also told her, I'm a spontaneous guy so I don't do rehearsals or anything like that…

But, what did this person expect? Contacting me, they had to know who I was and what my method is all about. Freedom! Zen! Art! I mean, the only other student film I ever did was also for a student at USC. That was back in 1990. But, I never auditioned. He liked my headshot. We talked on the phone. I showed up and we filmed the movie. As the lead of his student film, he even gave me the first, single card credit above a couple of working, name actors that were also in the production. I thought that was nice. This, before I had pretty much done anything else. But, the production was free, it was Zen, it was great!

But, let's get to the point of all this… How you move through life sets the stage for what you will or will not achieve. How you perceive others sets the stage for your possible interaction with people, which then sets the stage for whom and what you will later encounter in life. If you base your life upon a supposed, predetermined perception of other people, then all of the truth and the naturalness of life and the truth of personality is lost. Meaning, you are projecting you onto that person. You are projecting your loves, your hates, your desires, your definitions onto another person. Mostly, what you are doing is basing what you believed, (which may or may not be true), onto the outer world. Thus, you are robbing all of the what could be—based upon undefined, unsubstantiated perceptions.

Yes, I know, no matter where you find yourself in life, a lot of people say a lot of things about other people. Certainly, a lot of people, all of whom have never met me, have said a lot of things about me. Be they positive or negative, many/most of those things are far from the truth. They don't me! They have never met me! How can what they are saying be considered, on any level, to be the truth? All they were doing was attempting to project their perception of me out to the world. I'm sure people have said things about you, as well.

But, the ultimately truth of life, the ultimate truth of personality, is that if you are projecting your perceptions, all you are doing is robbing the truth from what another person actually is—who they actually are. For this reason, it is far better to simply allow a person to exist in their own truth while you do not attempt to project anything onto that truth.

I'm sure I could never be what that young filmmaker had hoped I would be, as they (apparently) wanted me to do things their way. But, their way is not my way. My way is not their way. Your way, may or may not be my way, but the only way we can ever know is if we personally interact. Then, perceptions/projections are lost and interpersonal truth is revealed.

Turn off perceptions and projections. Let the truth live.

      *   *   *
                14/Oct/2017 07:37 AM

The mistakes that mess up our lives are usually made by us.

But, how often do we blame ourselves?

*   *   *
13/Oct/2017 01:52 PM

If it's just not worth it, it's just not worth it.

* * *

13/Oct/2017 01:50 PM

Fixing your negative karma is easy, you just have to try. Do you? If you don't, blame no one but yourself when you experience the repercussions.

The Thing You Will Never See
12/Oct/2017 02:12 PM

I was flashing back to this commercial I did early in my career in the film industry. I think it was in '91. It was for Fanta soda and they had me riding my Harley around Hollywood.

I never saw that commercial, however. Though it was obviously a big production, it was shown in South America and they never gave me a copy. I would have liked to have seen it though.

Early in my career I did a lot of international commercials. I think it was due to my long blonde hair as that is how the world wanted to depict young, modern California at the time.

There were a few other international commercials I did, in that same era, that I also never saw. For Pepsi (Mexico) I was the father, next to my wife, as we picked up our young daughter at the airport. There was one for Budweiser (Europe) where I walked through the stands, during a baseball game, carrying a Bud. One for Vidal Sassoon (Asia) where I was a model having his hair done. One for Coke (Latin America) where I was a biker. One for Burger King (shown somewhere) where I was a dock worker. Some commercial for something, somewhere, where I walked off my private jet, all rock starred out, carrying a guitar… Never saw any of them…

I did a few TV shows like that, as well. Back then, if you didn't see it when it was on, you didn't see it. There was no On Demand and if the TV show didn't grow in fan popularity there was never a VHS or DVD release. So gone, I guess? I will never see my performances. Though I would have liked to.

Now, today, everyone has cameras. It happens all the time, people are taking pictures of me, you, anybody… I'm not really a fan of that style of behavior, but what can I do?

So, there are all these pictures of me out there somewhere. Pictures, I will never see. And, think about all of the surveillance footage that is shot in this day and age. Cameras are everywhere, photographing everything. This footage will probably exist forever, somewhere. Somewhere, we will never see...

Maybe a year ago, I wrote a blog about the fact that I was the last person who remembers my father. As he died fifty years ago, and though he had a lot of friends, did his military service during World War II, established a popular restaurant, was the manager of a major concert/sport facility, and so on, all the people who knew him are dead. I'm all that's left. The only one who remembers him. You will never see him.

This morning, I thought about my uncle. As he was a professional boxer during the 1930s, I looked him up on-line using his boxing name. I had done this a few years ago but found nothing. This time, I did find a site that had scanned a page from the boxing chronicles of that era where it listed his bouts and his knocks out. I thought that was cool. But again, I'm the last person who remembers him. Just like my father, he did his time in military service during the war, he had a lot of friends, but he chose to never get married. He just had girlfriends. So, he never had any children. I'm the last one who even remembers the name he boxed under. He was a good guy but you will never know him.

How much of life is like this? How many of the people that you know, will you end up being the only one that remembers them? How many people will remember you? And, why will they remember you?

Life is this fleeting illusion where the things that matter to you or me, matter only to you or me. The people that we care about; we are the only ones that care.

Do you care about my father? Do you care about my uncle? Do you care about me? Probably not. And, who cares about you? How can you care about a person when you do not even know that person? And here—this is where we find the ultimate illusion of life. It is all simply a photograph that will fade with time—lived and experienced but once it is lived and experienced the memories of those experiences and those emotions fade as time passes—emotions only felt by those who had a reason to feel those emotions.

Most of life is based upon a life lived and then the things you remember but most of things you will never see again.

Writing Reviews About Life
12/Oct/2017 07:09 AM

In this blog, it is kind of like me writing reviews about life. For those of you who read this blog you know I discuss my life experiences, my interpretations of life, the way in which I view human consciousness, and the way I hope people will understand they can live their life from a more pure, whole, and enlightened perspective.

Many people question why don't I charge for this blog or put it on of those sites where they run ads and thereby I would make money from these writings—as there are obviously a lot of them. But, that is far too disingenuous for me. Sure, we all need money to live. And hey, you can give me some money if you want to. ☺ But, if you are thinking what you are thinking based upon the perspective of charging money for it all that makes you is a business person not an individual operating from a space of Pure Thought.

I know there are many people out there who do make their money by discoursing about whatever or discussing and reviewing the thoughts and creations of others. But, as I have often stated, that is a person functioning from a basis of ego, believing that they possess the internal intelligence to rightfully evaluate the ideas, philosophies, and artistic creations of others. But, all they are doing is casting their opinion and their thoughts about someone or something, while presenting them as if they are facts. Which they are not.

Do you ever watch the talking heads on the news networks when they are evaluating the actions of politicians? One day they assume one thing, the next day the next. And moreover, how often are the completely wrong about the outcome that out comes? This is what reviews do; speculate. But, speculation is never based in truth or fact. Yet, some of these people make money from what they believe. But, if what they believe is wrong and what they say is false, where does that leave humanity? It leaves humanity stuffed full of a bunch of the key word of the day, *"Fake News."* Believing the falsity of one person's mind.

Thus, and therefore, I steer clear of all that kind of nonsense for all these people do is rationalize what they are saying and why they are saying it, when the real reason they are allowed to be saying it at all is that they are getting paid based upon ego driven evaluations. This is not a karmically pure space to operating from. And, what happens when the tax man comes to call?

At the heart of all true spirituality and at the essence of living a good life is existing in a space where what you do negativity affects no one. If your ideas hurt anyone, for any reason, if they are false by any stretch of the imagination, you have no right to be getting paid for them.

Give freely. Be free.

*   *   *

11/Oct/2017 06:50 PM

If you compliment or support the person who is negative, critical, or judgmental all that does is allow their ego to grow in their own self-righteous superiority.

There is nothing superior about negativity, criticalness, or judgement. These are all the signs of the person who is afraid to look at themselves so they cause the focus to be guided elsewhere.

When You're Secure in Yourself
11/Oct/2017 02:54 PM

Each of us, as we pass through life, will undoubtedly encounter a naysayer or two—those who speak badly about us. But, why does someone do this? Why do they behave in this manner? Why? Because they are not secure in themselves. They are not whole, complete, or self-actualized enough to realize that by speaking negatively about someone/anyone, for any reason, all it does is make themselves look weak, bad, and a purveyor of negativity.

Someone who says something bad about you, whether it is true or not, may feel they have all kinds of interpersonal reasons for doing so. They may be angry at you. They may not like you. They may just want to make you look bad so they spread altered truths and/or falsehoods about you. Whatever their logic, it does not dismiss the fact that they are not a complete enough person to step beyond their own ideological characterizations of who or what they think you are. Thus, they want to spread their belief about you out to others. They do this, in order to influence other people's opinions about you.

Certainly, everywhere we look, we can find people who listens to and embraces this level of character assignation. Why do they do this? Again, just like the naysayer, they are not whole and complete onto themselves to the degree where they have the interpersonal strength to steer away from this style of rhetoric. Thus, they become sucked into the melodrama that was created by one person's opinion or reaction to who or what they believe that you are.

Do you do this? Do you listen to other people's definitions and proclamations about a specific person or persons? If you do, do you ever contemplate why you do this? What drags you into this system of belief propagated by one, outspoken, person? Do you ever question, *"Why do I listen to other people's opinions about a person?"* Do you ever ask yourself, *"Why don't I investigate, interact with that person, and then form my own opinion?"*

Many people's lives are lived via what they hear and, thus, believe; spoken from the mouths of other people. But, this is not a <u>whole</u> level of living life. This is simply you, passing through your life, allowing other people to provide you with their interpretations of other people. Thus, you are not living your life at all. You are allowing your life, and the thoughts that make up your life, to be supplied by someone else.

Be more than the person who judges other people. For why does anyone judge anybody? Because they do not want people to look too closely at who, what, or why they are.

If you hear negative words being spoken about someone, either interrupt the person and stop them or walk away. Find your own meaning in life. Define your own definitions. From this, all you live, all you encounter, all you believed will be defined by no one but you. This is how to live a whole and complete, self-actualized life.

* * *

11/Oct/2017 07:24 AM

The moment you turn off the flame things start cooling down.

All You Can Do is Never Do It Again
11/Oct/2017 07:07 AM

Have you ever had one of those experiences where you go into a restaurant and you pay a lot of money for something and it either makes you sick or it is just not very good? You swear I will never eat that again! I do that a lot with the breakfast sandwiches at Starbucks. As I go to Starbucks most every day, and there they are, an easy way to get my breakfast on. But, they are just not very good! Every time I eat one, I am thinking, *"Why am I eating this?"*

In terms of the fast food, I used to like to drive through McDonalds in morning, enroute to my road trips, (of which I take a lot), and grab a Sausage McMuffin Combo with Coffee. But, then their prices went through the roof and the way they take your order just got so stupid, that it's just wasn't worth it anymore.

The thing is, most companies do what they do and there is really nothing you can do about it except not go to them if you don't like what's going on. They don't care about what the create, what they sell, or the impact it is having on the greater whole as long as they are making money.

People also do bad things that leave a bad taste in your mouth. And, most people do not care enough to look at themselves, look at the overall impact they are having on others and, thus, on themselves farther down to the line. Thus, they do not even think about changing as long as they are getting along or getting over.

This is where the personal interplay of caring mindfulness comes into the human spectrum as a pathway for evolving human consciousness. What do you do? What do you create? What impact does what you create have on others? What impact will what you do and what you crate do to your life as you pass through your lifetime? Do you ever think about this? If you don't, all that occurs is that you leave a lot of people with a bad taste in their mouth as you have evoked a negative experience in their life. If you have even done this to one person, you have done it to one too many.

Each of us has done bad things and perhaps created negative events in the life of another person. Some of us have done this way more than others. But, it is what you do after the fact that ultimately defines you as a human being. It is what you fix as oppose to what you break that will be the definition of your life.

So, what do you do when you have dished out that bad meal? Do you keep making the same receipt as long as it is easy and cost-effective? Or, do you care enough to care and change up your game plan? We all make mistakes in life. We all eat that bad meal at a restaurant. But, all you can do is to never do it again.

Reaching Out to Someone
10/Oct/2017 01:52 PM

    Have you ever reached out to someone via the internet and you were very sorry that you did as the interaction went in totally a different direction than you thought that it might? I don't know what it is, but at least for me, this has been the case more times than not. I don't know... I'm a nice, easy going guy. But, everyone else???

    This has happened to me several times when I have found a piece of art that I really liked, I bought it, and then found that the artist had a website or something so I contacted them to ask questions about the particular piece. In more than few cases, they were insulted that anyone would even think about selling their art, let alone that maybe I found it in a thrift store, at a flea market, or an estate sale. In a couple of cases they were so unpleasant and belligerent that I offered to give them back their work, minus the cost of shipping, of course. None of them ever took me up on this offer, however.

    Today, I had an interesting experience following this same vein of life interaction.

    To tell the story... A few days ago someone told me that someone had made a music video using footage from the *Roller Blade Seven* and live footage from the band Skinny Puppy and put it up on YouTube. I watched it and it was pretty good—interestingly creative. Me... I just assumed that it was done by the band themselves. I mean, who else would do something like that? So, I sent them a short email, via their website, telling them I thought it was pretty cool and I would put a link to it up on my website; which I did.

    This was a couple of days ago... Today, I got a marginally rude email from the leader of the band asking me if I was trying to promote my movie by using their music. WHAT! I, of course, was not! Everybody talks about *Roller*

Blade Seven. It needs no publicity. So, I guess the music video was just made by some fan of Skinny Puppy and the *Roller Blade Seven* who did the mashup.

Anyway… Life is interesting… I guess I should not have heads-up'd the band to the fact that the video was out there. At least that would have saved any hard feelings being born.

I don't know… Life in this digital age is interesting. In many ways it's really not too different than sending a letter in the days of the long ago and the far-far away. It's just a lot quicker and a lot less thought out. Mostly, it just seems that people have become very reactive instead of thinking about all of the goings-on that take place in the mind and the heart of other people.

Maybe I've finally learned my lesson about contacting people. Hummm ??? I don't know. ☺

Making Life Easier
08/Oct/2017 07:25 AM

Outside of where I have my computers set up there is a patio. On the patio, I have some succulent cacti. In the mornings, I watch as the humming birds come by and get their breakfast from the flowers that are blooming on the cacti. Sometimes in the afternoon, I watch as a bee or two stops by. Though I, of course, love plants, I really like to provide a service to the world's creatures in any small way that I can. I want them to know about a place where they can come by and find an easy meal. I want to make their life easier.

How about you? Do you try to make my life easier? Do you try to make anyone's life easier? Do you ever go out of your way, step outside of yourself, and do something so someone will have an easier road as they walk through life?

If we can step outside of ourselves, if we can take our mind's away from ourselves long enough to understand that other people are people. And, just like us, they too need a helping hand. From this, we can find the motivation to actually DO. Do something for someone else that will help them. And, from this doing, the world can become better one person's life at a time.

Many people do not think about anyone but themselves. Others think about people, but only the one's they directly care about. Maybe they want to make their life easier. But, they dismiss the fact that they can make someone's life, that they do not personally know, better by doing some small thing, some small gesture so just a bit of the something that person must deal with is partially removed. They are wrong. You can help by doing even the smallest of things.

Really, try it! Try to make the life of some person, some creature, some life form, some something easier.

Believe me, from this action, everything, everywhere becomes just a little bit better.

What Do You Consider Art?
08/Oct/2017 07:24 AM

As I've spent most of my life as an artist of one type or another, I've spent a lot of time thinking about art. In my earlier years, I did a lot research and reading into the various philosophies behind art and the motivations for and thereof. But, what I have basically concluded is that each person has their own unique interpretation as to what is and what is not art.

In any case, a few weeks ago I was in a thrift store and I came upon this beautiful 8-Track player/recorder from the mid 1970s. I had no idea if it worked or not. But, did I really care? It was beautiful. The only problem was, they were asking $49.99 for it, which is a fairly high price to be asked by a thrift store. I saw the manager walking around. She was a youngish Latina woman, who was quite full of pride due to her position. Her emissive attitude kind of made me smile. Anyway, I asked her if she would be willing to negotiate the price. She firmly said, *"Once I price something, that is the price."* Again, I smiled.

The price was high so I walked out of the store and went next-door to the office supply store which is why I was actually in the shopping center in the first place. I got what I needed but I couldn't get the 8-Track deck out of mind. I went back in and bought it. Yeah, it was a bit expensive for something that may or may not work. Yeah, the manager was less than cordial. But, with the deck in my hand, as I walked towards the cash register, I passed by her and said, *"I couldn't let it go…"* She smiled.

As I put the deck in my truck it made me think about art. I mean $50.00 for a piece of art is nothing. …A cheap price to pay. And, to me, here it was, an 8-Track deck from the 70s and a model I had never seen before. Art! It was definitely art!

So, for each of us we define what is or what is not art in our own mind. You may think I'm nuts believing that an 70s 8-Track deck is art. But, to me, it is true beauty. I have it over on my stereo rack next to my TV and whenever I see it, it makes me happy remembering a time gone past.

Art. It is such a personal interpretation.

* * *
07/Oct/2017 07:39 AM

How many of your facts do you know that you know?

How many of your facts do you confirm?

How many things do you repeat simply because you heard it somewhere from someone?

Does it bother you that you don't check your facts?

Does it bother you when you say something that turns out to not be true?

What do you do about the false knowledge that you spread?

What do you think the false knowledge you spread does to the world as a whole?

The Bigger Question is, Why Do You Care?
05/Oct/2017 01:19 PM

People spend a lot of time thinking and talking about things outside of themselves. Whether it is discussing what they think about a particular person, a sport's team, a music group, a movie, or a religious figurehead, whenever this style of dialogue occurs the discussion is moved away from Self. When the discussion is moved away from Self, the individual does not have to study who they are, what they are, and why they behave the way the behave. Thus, all sense of rising interpersonal human consciousness is lost to the mundane.

At the heart of all advancing mindfulness is a person's ability to study themselves. From this study, they are allowed the opportunity to raise their level of awareness, take control over their mind, and guide themselves towards become a better, more whole, human being. For those who spend their time disregarding this fact and losing themselves to monotonous patterns of thinking, they lose any chance they have of rising above the commonplace and moving themselves towards a deeper understanding of Self and universal knowledge.

Taking control over one's self is not easy. In fact, it is one of the hardest things that any person can accomplish. Removing one's self from this task is easy, however, as there are a million things out there to distract you. There are a million people, saying a million things, all designed to keep you from looking within. Everywhere you turn you will find someone attempting to drag you into the discussion of the mundane and keeping you from turning within, developing a highly defined mind, and moving yourself towards the higher mind and the betterment of all instead of simply focusing on what somebody thinks about some one or some thing.

This is your life. You are the only person who can take control over it and decide to make yourself something more. So, why do you care about something that does not truly effect your overall evolution? Why do you waste your time thinking about it? Why do you waste your time discussing it?

What Are You Giving Me?
05/Oct/2017 08:22 AM

People spend much of their life taking. They are happy to receive gifts, they are happy to get what they want, but they spend very little time thinking about what they can give to others. This is especially the case if they do not like, love, or personally know a specific individual.

People also spend a lot of their time thinking about, planning, and devising a method to get what they want. They may work and save their money in order to fulfill their desire of getting some, something. But again, this goes to the sourcepoint of getting and receiving. This action has very little to do with giving.

Think about this… How much of your time do you spend thinking about what you can give a specific somebody? Even if you love them, even if you are in a relationship with them, in most cases you are only thinking about giving them something they may want because by making them happy they give you something in return; i.e.: a relationship, love, a life definition because you have them in your life. Very little of what you do, for anybody, comes from the pure sense of giving. And, this is sad. This is where many of the world's problems begin.

There is the other side of the issue, as well. How many times has somebody given you something that they many have thought you wanted but you did not want at all. This happens a lot at Christmas, Hanukkah, and birthdays. People think they must give you a gift. But, if they do not understand the true inner you, they give you something that you may not even want. Yet, you must pretend that you like it. Is this giving at all?

People take and people make from what you have done in your life—from what you have created. Have you ever had the experience of somebody taking credit for something that you did? Have you ever had the experience of somebody making money from one of your creations? Have you ever had the experience of somebody taking a free ride from money you earned or money you spent? Did they appreciate any of those unintentional gifts? Probably not. Again, people take but people do not think about giving.

Whether it is from the music we like to listen to, the books we like to read, the spoken words we find inspiration from, or the movies and the TV shows we like to watch, we owe the creators of those entities the gift of giving them something. Why? Because without them, that music would not exist, that book would not have been written, those words left unspoken, that movie would not have been created, and so on... Do you ever think about this? Do you ever consciously try to give that creator anything? Probably not. Most people don't. But, it doesn't have to be that way.

Now, think about this... What do you prefer, getting what you want or giving what someone else wants? I believe if we look around the world, if look to the people we have interacted with as we have passed through our life, if we look to ourselves, the answer to that question is obvious. But, it does not have to the be that way. You can give. You can care enough to give. You can be conscious enough and compassionate enough to be able to step outside of your selfish realm of need and think about someone else and what they may want. You can care enough to go out of your way and actually give.

Try it. Give to those you love. Give to those you like. Give to those who have given something to your life. Give to those people you don't even know. Believe me when I tell you not only will your life become better, everything will become better.

Blaming Others Before You Blame Yourself
05/Oct/2017 08:16 AM

Have you ever encountered the situation where somebody does something really messed up to you and then, instead of owning their responsibility in it, they blame you? I think many of us have encountered this type of behavior as we have passed through life.

Who does this and why do they do it?

First of all, the person who behaves in this manner does not have a strong definition of Self; i.e., they hide from the truth about themselves and/or they want to be seen as something more than what they truly are. Thus, they lie.

Secondarily, the person who behaves in this manner does not care about anybody but themselves and how they are perceived, because if this were not the case, they would be man (or woman) enough to step up and say, *"I'm sorry. What can I do to fix what I have broken?"* But, as they are so locked into their misguided sense of Self and entitlement all they think about is themselves. Thus, they do not care about any damage they have evoked.

I think back to this incident that happened to me awhile back when I had this horrible neighbor. I don't know if you've ever had a really bad neighbor. ...I hope you haven't. But, the problem is, when you live in a big city, the chances of it happening are more probable.

Anyway, this guy was loud and rude. He destroyed the whole community. He believed himself to be some sort of pseudo spiritual teacher and he would go online and broadcast his borrowed knowledge to anyone who would pay to listen him while loudly spilling his words outwards to the entire neighborhood. When he wasn't doing that, he was so emotionally out of control that he would stomp on the floor screaming, *"Fuck me, fuck me, fuck me and mine,"* over and over and over again. I actually have him on tape doing this. Really a spiritual person, right? It was really hell for everyone around him. I tried to be nice. I tried to be understanding. I tried to be forgiving. I didn't report him to the police. I didn't sue him. But, when I finally complained about him to the community management, they showed me a letter of complaint that he had written about me. Me... OMG... I'm the quietest guy in the world. I meditate okay...

Now, years later, when I look back, I know a couple years of my life was damaged by this man. (Moving isn't cheap). He did hurt my life. He did hurt the life of all those people living around him. But, instead of saying, *"Sorry,"* he wrote a letter of complaint to take the focus off of himself and what he had done. Unbelievable... But, think how many people behave in this manner. Do you?

This is the ideal example of how people, who are based in an altered sense of Self, hurt the lives of others and they do not care. He wanted to blame me instead of looking at all of the damage he had created. He didn't want anyone else to know the truth about all the damage he created so he tried to deflect his responsibility. Yet, he did it. He made a choice and he hurt the lives of others. What is the karma for that? What is the karma for not taking responsibility for damaging the life or lives of someone else? What is the karma for not apologizing?

I have encountered other situations like this in my life. Where people, based upon whatever misguided sense of direction they possess, have decided to spread falsities and misnomers out to the world about me. For some reason, they felt they had the right to take what I had created or talk about me without even knowing me. Like I always say, *"Ask me first..."* But, no one ever does.

The fact of life is, if someone wants to go after you, if they don't like you for whatever reason, there is very little you can say or do that will change their mind. Your words will only give them new inspiration to turn your reality into something negative. And, here lies one of the root causes for all of the problems with the world, people believe they know but they do not know anything…

I talk about myself here because I have substantiated examples. But, I have sadly known people have who have been forced into taking their own life because people have done bad things to them; not only on this physical plane of existence but on places like the internet, as well. Some people are not strong. Some people do not have a good support network. Some people are all alone. Then what? What is the karma for some person hurting someone to that degree?

And, this goes to the bigger issue… Do you ever think about what you do before you do it? Do you ever think or care about what may happen to a specific person because of what you do or say? And, if you are actually trying to hurt someone by what you say or do, what do you think will be the closing definition of your life?

Life is fragile. Some people's lives are very fragile. If you don't care about what you are doing to their life—if you don't think about the bigger implications of your actions, what will be your final karma?

Ultimately, what I am saying here is that, you really should be Whole enough onto yourself to understand that we all make mistakes, we all do things that we should not do, we all (maybe unintentionally) hurt other people. Though you should never perform any of these actions intentionally, if you do, you should fix them and not hide from them.

Moreover, think about other people first. Think about how the words you are saying will affect them. Think about how what you are doing is affecting the next-door neighbor. In other words, care. Care enough to care. Care enough to not allow you ego, your out of control emotions, your lack of Self to drive you to do something that may the hurt the life of someone else.

Always help. Never hurt.

* * *
05/Oct/2017 06:44 AM

If what you are saying, if what you are doing is hurting someone, you are doing the wrong thing.

This is the mistake that many people make. They believe they have the right to say or do whatever they want. They believe they have impunity. They are wrong. All words, all actions have consequences.

The wise person say nothings negative, does nothing negative and simply sits back and studies the reactions to the actions.

* * *

04/Oct/2017 03:31 PM

Somebody said something. You heard it. You believed it. But, what if what they said was wrong? That means you have spent a certain percentage of your life believing a lie.

* * *
03/Oct/2017 12:11 PM

Are you strong enough to stand up against the masses when they are saying or doing something negative to someone or something?

* * *

03/Oct/2017 11:59 AM

Do you ever do anything differently?

* * *
03/Oct/2017 11:55 AM

It's easy to voice your opinion when the person you are voicing your opinion about has no way to respond.

*   *   *
03/Oct/2017 11:54 AM

No life is solely defined by what is expected.

* * *
03/Oct/2017 05:57 AM

If you are waiting for someone to approve of what you are doing you will forever be waiting.

If you are doing things hoping someone will like what you are doing you will forever be doing.

As long as you are seeking approval outside of yourself you will never be whole onto yourself—you will never be who you truly are.

We Will All Be Forgotten
02/Oct/2017 04:25 AM

Periodically, I mention the fact that in my lifetime I have watched as some of the most influential martial artists have passed away and all but been forgotten. These were people who truly made a contribution to the evolution of the martial arts.

It is important to note that it was not until the twentieth century, with the advent of mass media, that it became possible for a person, in their own time, to readily contribute to the wide-spanning understanding and evolution of the martial arts or anything else for that matter. A few people took up this banner, spread their understanding, but then they were gone and quickly all they had contributed was lost to the hands of time.

This is also the case with spiritual teachers. Perhaps a person came on the scene with a unique message that came to be embraced. They taught what they but they, as we all will do someday, passed away. Then, that person and their message was quickly forgotten.

If you want to look at the more celebrity driven realms, think to that TV show that you really liked as a kid. What happened to the star of that show? In many/most cases, those actors were never seen again.

Many people, as they pass through life, seek a means to get their ideas, their name, or their face out to the public eye. They may do this due to vanity, ego, or the belief that they have something unique and special to offer. Whatever the motivations may be, it is one person stepping to the pulpit, presenting a platform, and in some cases, that person becomes noted for what they do or what they have to say. Though, in that moment, they may find students or followers; perhaps their ego or their bank account gets stroked, but the reality is, a person is only viable when they are alive. With very few exceptions as soon as they die, their teachings die.

Most people do not step to the pulpit. Most people simply live a simple life, going to work, while supporting a family. Thus, they may listen (for a time) to the talkers or the teachers of the world but their focus is on their survival and their family. This is why so few teachers/talkers remain viable after their passing. People have their own life and they only care about you as long as they have a reason to care about you.

For anyone who has ever owned a school of the martial arts, hatha yoga, or any other business for that matter, it is easily witnessed how the clientele come and go. People have an interest and then due to change of time, change of mind, change of heart, change of life focus, or change of financial circumstances they move away. Thus, nothing, in the life of the person at the forefront of the conversation is permeant—nothing last forever.

It is important to keep this in mind as you pass through life: as a student, a follower, or as the teacher. In your life, you may find nourishment from what someone else is giving. In your life, you may find sustenance by what you have to give. But, nothing last longer than your life. When you are dead, you are dead. Don't fool yourself. We will all be forgotten.

* * *
02/Oct/2017 04:24 AM

You have done something that has hurt someone.

Do you care?

Do you try to repair the damage?

In these answers; here lies the definition of your life.

What Makes You Think That I'm Not a Muslim?
01/Oct/2017 06:09 AM

There is this gate in the old city of Jerusalem that I decided to exit via last week. One of the Israeli military guards, that carries an AK47 around their neck—that are everywhere, stopped me and said, *"Muslims only."* Now, I knew that this was a fact about this gate—that they only allow Muslims to enter and exit through it. Why I don't really know. I guess I could do some research and figure it out. But, I thought I would give it my best shot. But, when he told me that, it struck a strange chord in me. What I wanted to question was, *"What makes you think that I'm not a Muslim?"*

A little backstory here... When I was seventeen I was initiated into the Sufi Order, which is a sect of the greater Muslim faith. So, the fact is, yes, I am a Muslim. Now, I didn't want to get into a whole debate with the guy, breaking out my Arabic and exclaiming, *"La ilaha illallah Muhammadur Rasulullah,"* or anything like that. But, I was judged by how I look. And, yeah sure, I get it, I guess I don't look like your average Muslim. But, looks can be deceiving. I'm sure there are a lot of Muslims out there with blonde hair. But, more than that, why does there need to be a definitive definition?

You know, when I was growing up spirituality was clearly one of my primary focuses. When I came up, where I came up, and who I came up with, the acceptance and the merging of the various religions was the norm. In my line of Sufism, Pir-O-Murshid Hazrat Inayat Khan was the instigating factor and the man who introduced Sufism to the West in the early twentieth century. Though many teachers of my era were exclaiming that all religious should be honored, he said an interesting thing. And, I am paraphrasing... He said, *"If a Christian asks you what religion you are, you say I'm a Christian. Is a Jew asks you what religion you are, you say I'm Jewish. If a Muslim asks you what religion you are, you say I'm Muslim, and so on."* Meaning, that in Sufism all religions are respected and embraced. And, that is how I feel. I believe I am a part of all of those religions.

Certainly, in this modern day, with all of the craziness going on around the world, religion has become a very divisive factor. But, that is all personal choice. It doesn't have to be like that. It doesn't have to be the, *"I am this, you are that. Mine is better than yours."* It can just be acceptance where no gates are closed to those of other faiths.

The truth is, most people do not wear their religion on their sleeve. I was at the mall a couple of weeks ago, here in the L.A. area, and I noticed that this one guy who was operating one of those kiosks got out his prayer rug, laid it down, and was praying. This is something that the practicing Muslims do. Pray at a specific time each day. I thought that was great. Here is this man, with all of the religious tensions simmering around the world, especially against Muslims but, there he was, owing who and what he was right in the heart of a shopping mall.

I think the big question is, *"Why are you what you are and why do you believe what you believe?"* Moreover, why do you/why do any of us, have to draw boundaries between us and anyone else just because of what we believe?

So, what makes you think that I'm not a Muslim?

*   *   *
30/Sep/2017 06:17 AM

We all have to live with the decisions we make.

* * *

30/Sep/2017 05:01 AM

What are you going to do today that helps someone other than yourself?

The Presidential Suit
29/Sep/2017 07:18 AM

I was watching one of those shows on TV last night about people who revamp and remodel houses. The main players were considering redoing this massive mansion. It was one of those places where the owners planned to go in a very gaudy direction. It set me to remembering…

I had flown into Manila in the mid 1980s and I headed for the Hilton where I had booked a room. My plane arrived at night and when I got to the hotel they told me that they were fully occupied but they would promote me to a suite. Okay… The bell man took my suitcase and myself up the elevator to the top floor. The elevator opened exposing the presidential suite which took over the entire top floor. Wow! After the bell man left, I walked around. It was one of those ridiculously opulent places with gold bathroom fixture, mirrors housed in gold frames, gold bed post, gold sheets and bed spreads, and the like. In other words, it was beyond gaudy. I was later informed that it was the place that then President Ferdinand Marcos would take women when he needed a getaway. The suit was so massive that I literally found myself getting lost walking around. Sleeping there the first night was a very-very weird experience.

I expected that I was only going to be there one night, but night two and then night three went by and they did not move me out. I thought maybe they forgot about me.

Having that suite definitely set all of those young man fantasies into motion about finding the right girl to take up there and make it look like I was a total player. But, I knew the rules of the game all too well by that point in my life and the kind of girl that I could have easily found in Manila to bring to that suite was probably not the kind of girl that it would have been in my best interest to allow into the presidential suite. So, the offers I had I passed on.

On the forth morning I got a phone call. They wanted to demote me. Thus, the bell man took me down to a regular sized room. Going from the presidential suite to a regular sized hotel room was one of the most demeaning experiences I had ever encountered. As you can imagine, it was such a let down. I sat there on the bed in that room, questioning all of the realities of life, my life, and how people live a certain way and why.

That afternoon I got a telex from my girlfriend in Bangkok. She asked me to catch a flight and come and see her. Thinking of my room, or the lack thereof, I immediately agreed.

Now, this was obviously before the days of the internet and I had to actually go to the airline office and buy a ticket: Manila to Bangkok. The sad/funny part about all this was, while in the office I met this beautiful young lady who obviously liked what she saw in me. We got talking and I joking asked her if she wanted to come to America with me. She, of course, said she did and immediately assumed I was proposing to her. She said she wanted to come to America with me but we should get to know each other a little bit better first so I can make sure that I liked her. This, of course, made me smile… But, I was on my way to Bangkok. A journey that ended in becoming a complete mess. If only I had met that girl from the Philippines a couple of days earlier when I had the presidential suite, you never know what would have occurred… ☺ But, I never saw her again.

So, what does this all tell us about life? I don't know? There are a lot of ways you can read it. I told you the whole story, so you can come to your own conclusions. But, if nothing else it does demonstrate the way some people live, which causes other people to aspire to that gaudy end goal. But, what is the price to get there? What is the motivation to want to be there? And, how do you pay the price to live at that level of physical existence? What is the cost of that ticket? What does living at that level do to your life, your karma, and the lives of those you interacted with while rising to that level of affluence? …History tells us what happened to President Marcos.

Let Your Hair Grow AKA Why Conform to Normality?
28/Sep/2017 11:25 PM

I remember as I was driving along PCH (Pacific Coast Highway) in Manhattan Beach one evening, right at the end of the 1980s and there was this DJ, Dusty Street, talking to the band, The Cult, on her radio show. This was right before they were to break big. Now, I had known of this band when I was living in the UK as they evolved from the Southern Death Cult to The Death Cult and now to The Cult. She asked them about hair and mentioned how she was telling everyone to cut their long hair. They all totally disagreed. *"No! Let your hair grow,"* they exclaimed!

Me too! I agreed with this statement. I mean why fall into the norm? Why fall into the easy and the accepted by society? Me, Scott Shaw, I suggest, take the next three years and let your hair grow! See what it brings you.

There is something very freeing and very unleashing about just letting your hair grow.

Now, I imagine that most of you who read this blog do not understand the semblance of a man (or a woman) letting their hair grow. At the time when I grew up, a man with even the smallest appearance of having long hair was not even let into Disneyland. How messed up is that? As it was only a few generations ago when a man, having long hair, was the accepted norm. But, as time evolved, into this modern era, the normal became the accepted and that was that. Hair was gone. But, is the, *"That was that,"* right? No. It is just, that was that. But, society was so against us… In fact, I remember when I was about thirteen years old waking up to find that all of my long locks had been cut off by my mother as I was sleeping and it was laying there all around me on my pillows. All this, just to remove any form of freedom and self-evolution that I may have been embracing. Thus, just another form of control. …Controlling who you are.

So, this all goes to the bigger picture of who you are and why you are. I suggest that you remove yourself from all this control. Remove yourself from the who you are expected to be. Let yourself be free. Let your hair grow.

What Would You Do for Your God?
28/Sep/2017 05:35 AM

I recently watched the Martin Scorsese film, *Silence*. Now, this film could certainly be deconstructed in many ways but what it breaks down to is seventeenth century priest(s) having gone to Japan to convert the people and in doing so they are captured by the powers-that-be and eventually, at least pretend, to give up their faith. One may initially ask, is it the right thing to do at all to go to a foreign soil and try to covert the people to your religion? But, going far beyond that, people are believers. As people are believers, they believe. From this belief, they believe that other people should believe as they do. Yet, what would you do for your god? If you were held captive in a foreign land, with no hope of return, would you give up your belief? Or, would you die holding onto it?

The fact is, you will probably never be forced to answer that question. And, that is a good thing. In recent times, with the Islamic insurgence in the Middle East, we have witnessed, via the news, how some captives let go of their Christianity and embrace the Islamic faith. Yet, they too were executed. So, what did their belief or the lack there of prove?

Recently, I've been in Israel—with most of my time spent in Jerusalem. I really love Jerusalem. I go there wherever I can. It is truly one of the most holy cities on earth. It is a place where people truly embrace their religion. Everywhere you look, people wear their faith. Whether it is the Hasids, the various sects of the Muslim faith, onto the various Christian denomination, the people own what they believe. And, they do it, for the most part, right next door to one another. It is truly an inspirational sight.

But, there you are, in the middle of all of this faith; some people are laughing, some people are praying, most everyone, (at least the men), are smoking. It's funny, a couple of days ago this Hasid walks up to me after leaving his synagogue and asks me for a light for the cigarette he has hanging out of his mouth. *"Sorry, I don't smoke." "Damn it,"* he exclaims, as he goes in search of another match. This made me smile.

I mean, isn't the body supposedly the temple of the soul? Yet, there they are, the true believers, destroying their temple.

Most people believe. That's good. It gives them a purpose and a definition. It may even provide them with a code of conduct that they can follow. But, what would/what do most of these people do for their god. Though most would exclaim, *"Anything,"* this is probably not actually the case.

So, let's go back to the original premise of this piece. *"What would you do for your god?"* Think about it.

* * *

27/Sep/2017 04:50 AM

Prayer is asking for something.

Meditation is asking for nothing.

* * *
27/Sep/2017 04:48 AM

Have you ever noticed that the people who complain the loudest are also the laziest?

* * *

27/Sep/2017 04:44 AM

Is what you are saying a compliment or an insult?

If what you are saying is a compliment, you make friends and help the greater evolution of the world.

If what you are saying is an insult, you create enemies and offset the ongoing betterment of yourself and all things related to yourself.

Morality and the General Order of Things
27/Sep/2017 04:43 AM

When I had graduated high school and started my studies at the university level the first field that I choose as a major was philosophy. Having been drawn to Eastern, and to a lesser degree, Western Philosophy for most of my life, I felt this was the obvious choice for my course of study. That was until I found out that in academic philosophy a good portion of it is based upon mathematical equations, statistics, and the like. Only a small percentage of it is given over to the actual study of philosophic teachers and texts.

In any case, one of the first classes I took focused on the definition and the understanding of morality and how it affects the overall approach to and the definition it unleashes onto not only the individual but to society as a whole. For me, as a person who had always spent a lot of time contemplation this type of stuff, the class provided an opportunity to come to a clearer understanding of the why, the wherefore, and the way people approach life.

Do you think about what you do, why you do it, and how what you do affects your life and the life of those around you? I believe that most people do not. They just do. They just do to get what they want. And, they care not about the consequences of their actions to others.

Here lies the basis of morality. Do you have a clearly defined motivational factor for why you do what you do? And, do you care about the effect what you do has on one person or many? Maybe you do. Then you are a moral person. Maybe you don't. Then, that means that you are not a moral person. It is a very simple equation.

If you take the time to look around yourself and study the people you have known, you can see who bases their life on a moral code of conduct and who does not. If you take the time to study yourself, you can see if you base your own life upon a moral code of conduct or not. But, at the bases of all of this calculation is the question, do you care? Do you care about how what you are doing is affecting your life, the lives of those you know, and the lives of those that you don't know? And, will you change what you do because of this discovered fact.

So much of this world is defined by the actions of people who hold no true sense of morality. They want. They do. They take. They don't think. And, they don't care. But, is that a good place to be operating from?

The fact is, religion is one of the greatest sources of projected morality for this world and it has been this way across time. For it is from religion that people are guided towards becoming a better version of themselves. Certainly, religion has also been the cause of many negative emancipations from time immemorial but it has also been the place where the individual can find guidance on how to become a better person. But, you have to look for this guidance. You have to care about choosing morality over self-serving actions. The fact is, most people do not. Why bother; right? Joe over there does that, why can't I?

At the heart of your existence is what you choose to do and how you choose to behave. From this choice, you can invoke a legacy of goodness or selfishness. And, you can find people who will tell you that either one of these life choices is the right life choice for you. But, here lies the source of morality and how it shapes the life of the individual. Morality is a choice. Doing the right thing is a choice. Hurting no one by the actions you take is a choice. Helping people instead of being selfish is a choice. Giving is a choice, just as taking is a choice. The choice you make is all based upon the morality you embrace. What do you choose to do? Can you be more than a self-based person? Can you care enough to care about the other person first? Can you be a moral person?

If It's Not Recorded Did It Ever Happen?
27/Sep/2017 04:42 AM

There is this app on the iPhone that records how many steps you take each day. But, it only works when your phone is turned on. At least for me, sometimes I turn my phone off. ...Maybe I want to save the battery. Maybe I don't want to be disturbed. And, so on... The question is, if my steps are not being recorded did they ever happen—did I ever take them at all?

For some, they will say, of course you did. But, without proof, how can that fact be substantiated?

There used to be this chain of gyms around the Los Angeles area that had very nice indoor tracks. I belonged to them and virtually every day of the week I would go there and run three or four miles. And, this went on for twenty years or more. But, this was long before the iPhone so none of those miles were being recorded. Did I ever run those miles? I remember doing it. But, do I remember every step of those runs? Of course not. A few runs are memorable because something specific happened. Most, however, just fade into the blur of my mind. I know I did it. But, it is only me who remembers. Did they ever happen at all?

This is an important thing to contemplate as you pass through life. What, of what you have done, is being recorded? And, are these recordings the only thing that gives your life credibility and meaning?

For most, they pass from birth to death, doing what they do, without the means or the desire to take stock of their actions. They do, but they never think about what they do, why they are doing it, and how will what they are doing affect the overall definition of their life and their lives of those they interact with. How about you? Do you take stock of what you are doing and why you are doing it? Do you have any record of what you have done? And, if you do or if you don't, how does that calculation define who you are as a person and what contribution you have made to society?

Fame: Paid for by Others
15/Sep/2017 09:08 AM

    Recently, here in the L.A. area, there was this woman caught on security camera sneaking up behind an elderly lady who was shopping for groceries in one of those motorized carts and stealing her purse when she was not looking. The thief's face is plastered all over the news. I mean, how uncool is that? Stealing from an old lady. I'm sure the thief has all kinds of justifiable reasons, at least in her own mind, for doing what she did. But, stealing is just wrong. Now, the thief is famous. Famous for all the wrong reasons.

    Due to this news story, a local news crew decided to test the honesty of people so they put a purse on top of a car to see what would occur. Within about five minutes these two women snagged the purse, got into their car, and drove away. The news crew had put a GPS tracking devise inside the purse. So, when the women took off the news crew got into their car and followed them. The thieves apparently realizing they were being followed tried to get away but got caught in traffic. The news crew pounced. The thieves had even discovered the GPS device and put it in a drink they had apparently hoping to disable it. The news crew got them on camera making all kinds of excuses about everyone makes mistakes and so on… Now, these women are famous. Famous for all of the wrong reasons.

    First of all, if you know what you are doing is wrong, don't do it! Be strong enough—be moral enough to control yourself and don't do it!

    Secondarily, these were two incidents that were caught on camera. But, think how much thievery takes place all the time that is not caught on camera. Everybody who steals probably has a reason for doing it. But, stealing is not right. Taking anything from anybody for any reason that you do not own, that does not belong to you, is wrong. But, do you think it is wrong? Do you steal? Do you have a reason that you believe justifies your thievery?

And, here we get to the entire crux of this situation. If you don't care about other people, then you find reasons to steal from them. They are people too! What will occur to their life because you have stolen something from them? And, do you care?

Most people don't steal. But, the people who do steal, no matter at what level of larceny, are taking what is not theirs—what they did not earn. They are taking what was not willfully given to them. These people should never be honored at any level.

* * *
15/Sep/2017 07:23 AM

Your life is only as good as the goodness you unleash.

You Sound Like a Very Angry Person
15/Sep/2017 07:15 AM

Have you ever had one of those situations where you are passing though life and all of a sudden somebody blows up in your presence for seemingly no reason at all? They totally over react in a manner that in is not only inappropriate but quite surprising to you? Maybe you are the focus of their anger. Maybe you did something or said something that they did not like. Maybe it is somebody else that sent them into a rage. But, they go off. And, when they go off they drag others into their melodrama.

So many of people's and, on a large scale, the world's problems, are created by people who are internally angry.

Some people seemingly look for a reason to become angry. The are not sufficiently fascinated with life unless that have some reason to find their anger. Other people are just stewing under the surface. They are mad at some distance memory; a life situation that turned and shaped them into a person based upon rage. From this, the moment something goes in a manner that they do not like, they have a reason to explode. Yes, it may be justifiable in their own mind, but they rage and from this rage they impact not only their own life in a negative fashion but all those within earshot.

It is very uncomfortable to be around people like this for they damage the life and the life experience of all those who they force to encounter their anger. It is very uncomfortable to be the focus of the anger of a person's who basis their life upon this emotion because they have driven themselves into a rage based upon an altered personally defined sense of misplaced emotion.

What makes you angry? How do you act and how do you react to the emotion of anger?

One of the key factors to your life experience is how you cope with your anger. Anger is a human emotion.

Virtually all of us feel it from time to time. But, it is what you do with that emotion that defines you as a person and defines the impact of your life onto others. Do you control your anger or does it control you?

Another key factor of life is how you react to the anger instigated by others. Have you ever been the focus of someone's misguided anger? What did you do? How did you react? Did you allow that person who was angry to drag you into their melodrama?

Remember, anger is an emotion experienced by one person. But, that one person has the potential to drag others into experiencing a similar emotion.

People who base their lives upon undefined, uncontrolled anger, hope to drag others into their rage. In fact, though for the most part they have no defined understanding of what they are doing or why, they achieve some sort of internal self-satisfaction if they cause others to lose their peace. Thus, that raging person has gained the control over others that they do not have over their own life. They have forced their will onto another. From this, they gain a sense of meaningfulness. Certainly, this emotion is wrongly placed, but none-the-less, due to their lack of a refined sense of their higher self, they enjoy some level of suchness.

So, what does this all tell us? First of all, it tells us that if you are a person prone to bouts of rage, do what it takes and get yourself under control. For not only are you hurting your own life but you are damaging the life of others. And, if you think that it is okay to hurt the lives of others, (on any level for any reason), you are really lost. You really need help! Get it!

For those of you who find yourself being forcefully pulled into the mental wrath of another person, don't let them control you. You are more than that. Walk away if you can. Tell them to calm down if you can't. But, never let them control your actions based upon undefined rage.

I Used to Be Better
14/Sep/2017 01:43 PM

It's kind of interesting… I was asked to provide a painting for an upcoming art show. In the processing of deciding which one I was going to give the gallery, I happened on some of my much older works from the early 1980s. I could not help but be surprised. Though they are totally different from the style I evolved into painting, they are really-really good! In fact, some of them are so much better than a lot of my more recent work. I was shocked! I had totally forgotten about that person I used to be and the paintings I used to paint.

Maybe eight or nine years ago I decided to go through my rolls and rolls of painted canvas I had in my storage unit. When I did, I realized that there was a lot of those paintings that I did not like. Though I went against the wished of my lady, (who went through them with me), I destroyed maybe forty-five percent of my past paintings. Sure-sure, I had spent a lot of money on those very large canvases; many of them were as big as six foot by four foot and, in a couple of cases, even bigger. And yeah, the amount of paint that it took to paint those large canvases was not cheap. But, it was so freeing to remove myself from a definition of myself that I did not like. And yes, the art you create does define you as a person—just as what you do in your life: what you do with your life, what you say, and what you create defines you and what your existence means to humanity. Freeing, it was freeing…

But today, it was the total opposite experience. I looked at those painting and wondered what medium did I used, how did I get that style of brush stroke, and how could I go back in time?

I think it is important that, every now and then, we each take a long hard look at our past. Because who were are now is probably very different from who we were then. Sure, the then, and what we do in between, equals our now but sometimes we get sidetracked. Sometimes our vision of our self gets lost in the shuffle of life. Sometimes we need to look back and maybe reformulate our now by reevaluating who we once thought we were and who we once thought that we should become.

I'm Sorry
14/Sep/2017 06:58 AM

Have you ever had somebody do something to you that either hurt you, offended you, or damaged your life in some way and then they said, *"I'm sorry?"* Have you ever done something to someone else that either hurt them, offended them, or damaged their life in some way and then you said, *"I'm sorry?"* Have you ever had somebody do some bad something to you and they didn't even care enough to say anything?

"I'm sorry," always has struck me as a strange concept. Yes, it is the conscious thing to say to someone when you have done something wrong to them. Yes, it makes you feel somewhat better when someone acknowledges the fact that they have done something wrong to you. But, what does that statement actually change? What does it make any better? Does it remove any of the damage that was created by the action that caused someone to say, *"I'm sorry?"* No.

Now, some people—some very conscious people do something wrong to someone, they realize it, and then they set about on a course to repair the damage. A person who possess that mindset is very rare however. Do you follow that path of redemption? Most do not. At best, if a specific person cares enough to care at all, they think that saying, *"I'm sorry,"* rights their wrongs. But, it does not.

So, this is something to think about as you pass through life. If you do something wrong to someone, you should acknowledge it—you should care enough to care. But then, you should set about on a course to repair the damage. …Don't make excuses for your actions, don't justify your actions, don't try to turn the blame around on the other person, simply acknowledge and repair what you have done.

You can't make anything better if you don't try to make it better and, *"I'm sorry,"* is just meaningless words if you don't back that statement up with action.

* * *
13/Sep/2017 07:52 AM

If you are looking for something to criticize you can always find something to criticize.

* * *
13/Sep/2017 07:51 AM

So, you have done something that has hurt someone. Now what do you do?

Who You Owe What to and Why
13/Sep/2017 07:45 AM

Recently, I've been spending a lot of time in-negotiations regarding various film projects and it has once again been vividly brought to light all of the realities of who owns what and why. Very often in this blog I discuss the truth of Intellectually Property Rights and why things like Copyrights and Trade Marks are so important. But, it seems my words are only heard by the creator(s) of said properties. Everybody else wants to dance around the truth of these facts.

Having been formally involved in the film business for just shy of thirty-years, at this point in my life, I have witnessed a lot of things that people outside of the Hollywood game have no idea about. Yet, as the entertainment industry has evolved—primarily at the hands of the internet, people from across the globe have become players. But, players at what level? Most are not creating their own subject matter—their own art if you will. They are simply taking the product someone else envisioned and getting paid. ...Getting paid while the actual creators are not. Thus, a lot of negative karma is being created.

I think back to this one individual I met when I was very new to the industry. They had access to a lot of money, via the hands of an investor, and they rose to literally the top of the independent film industry. They said to me, way back when, *"If all this ends tomorrow, at least I will have lived what I have lived."* At that time, I thought that was a very profound statement coming from the mouth of a twenty-year-old. As stated, they went on to rise to literally the top of the game. But, they did it by cheating, stealing, deceitfully robbing the vision of other people. What happened to them? Utter destruction. I won't go into the details, but it was bad. Long ago I had given up on karma in the film industry until I saw it actualize with that person.

More than just that one person, I have seen it happen with others who followed a similar path. They lived high on the hog for a period, but then they feel hard—very hard…

I have told this to people… I have warned people about what is to come if you steal the creations and/or make your living off of the vision of others but no one listens. And, there is a reason for this. …Because they are gaining fame and they are getting paid.

The fact is, we all need money to survive. Most of us have to work at various jobs to achieve that money. Some make their money by being creative. It is rare, but it does happen. Most artists, poets, authors, musicians, and filmmakers are broke most of their life, however. Yet, they are living via their creativity (at all costs). And, to them that is a price worth paying.

Particularly in music, writing, and the film game there is a method to make money off of the creativity of others. Perhaps a person starts a company, takes what someone else has created, and sells it.

Now, selling comes in many forms. As things like books, CDs, and DVDs have fallen away, they do it via various methods on the internet. Some of these methods are considered legal, others are not. But, the key component to this money-making venture is that someone else, other than the creator, is the one making the money.

Via the internet there have been some people who have risen to their own fame via making money off of the conceptions of others. From Shawn Fanning and Sean Parker of Napster onto the people who take footage from people films and critique them online, people get famous, while making money off of the creations of others, but pay the actual creator no money for doing so. Thus, they are making a living off of the vision and toil of someone else. What do you think is the karma for that?

Certainly, the people who make their living in this fashion will argue about their rights to do so to the grave.

But, do they have any rights at all? They did not create the product, yet they are getting rich off of it? Do you not see the problem in this equation? They may have all kinds of misguided logic about why they can do it, but central to the calculation is them, one person, either making money or getting famous off of what they had nothing to do with creating.

If you are standing on the outside of this whole situation, it is easy to understand the logic of what I am saying. If you are viewing it from the stance of a creator, you totally understand. If, on the other hand, you are the person making money via what someone else has created, you will, no doubt, be upset by what I have written. But, ask yourself, *"Are you not making money and perhaps gaining fame off of the creation(s) of someone else?"* Now, ask yourself, *"What is the karma for that?"*

Moreover, if you are making your way through the world via the vision, the labor, or the creativity of someone else; what do you think you owe them? You owe the everything! Pay your debt!

100

Falsely Presented Reality
12/Sep/2017 08:39 AM

I forever find it curious when somebody takes it upon themselves to explain the life of somebody else to another person. Maybe they are attempting to tell them why a person does what they do, behaves as they behave, or makes the choices that sets their life into motion. They somehow believe that they possess all of the answers for and about that person; their life and their life choices. But, of course, they do not. How could they! They are not that person. They do not know the foundational factors of why the person thinks in the specific manner that they do. Yet, they attempt to explain that person, their motivations, and their life to others.

The fact is, there are a lot of people who possess the know-it-all mentality out there. Whether knowingly or not they feel they have the right to describe the mind(s) of others. Of course they do not, but none-the-less they speak as if they do. And, people listen…

Why do people listen? Because many people are not capable of thinking for themselves. …They choose to not think for themselves. They don't want to think. They don't want to do the investigative research into what they are thinking about. They simply want to be told how to think and what to believe as this non-thinking lifestyle/mindset is so much easier. From this, the people who think they know the answers step into the foreground and talk while others listen.

Have you ever had somebody describe you, your life, or the logic behind the choices you have made to someone else? Then, once you heard what they were saying you realized that all of these supposed facts about you were totally wrong. Yet, someone said them. Maybe one person, maybe many people believed what was being spoken. Now what? A lie about you is out there, presented as if it were the truth.

Turn this around... Do you ever present your beliefs about a specific person or persons to other people? Do you ever tell people who, what, and why another person believes, thinks, and/or makes the choices that they do? If you do, why do you do it? What makes you believe you have the insight to present your thoughts as facts?

In life, there is who you are and what you think. Then, there is the way people perceive who you are and what you think. But, the fact is, there is commonly a large dichotomy between the two.

The point of all this being, in life you can only be whole and true onto yourself. If you take the time to study yourself, you can come to intimately know yourself and why you do what you do. Many people don't do this, however. They don't study themselves. They just act, react, and talk. But, this is a very shallow place to live your life from.

One of the main things to realize as you pass though life is that you will never truly know another person. This is the case even if you have been in a long-term interpersonal relationship with them. And, this is certainly the case if you are not a part of a person's inner circle. Understanding this, you can frame your life with two factors of absolute knowledge. One, you can only know yourself. And, you can only do this if you acutely study yourself. Two, you can never truly know another person. If you are presenting facts about that person to the ears of others all you are doing is destroying the truth of reality by believe that you are the possessor of knowledge. You are not. You do not know them. Don't attempt to define them.

* * *
12/Sep/2017 06:51 AM

Embrace the perfection.

* * *
12/Sep/2017 06:50 AM

Some people don't wake up and smell their karma.

* * *

12/Sep/2017 06:49 AM

If somebody says something negative correct them and say something positive. Shift the paradigm and observe the reaction.

Pure Cinema Cinéma Pur
11/Sep/2017 10:42 AM

As I have been making movies for a lot of years by this point in my life, I forever find it interesting how people perceptive cinema. We all begin watching a particular movie with a concept of what we are getting into. This definition is based upon what we are told to expect. Then, we base our judgment of that particular cinematic production upon if our personal vision of what we were told to expect was met or not. *"I liked it." "I hated it!"* And, so on…

People have the tendency to project their own perspective onto whatever they are viewing. They have come to like a certain type of cinema so they base all of their viewing experience upon that belief. The problem with this formula is, however, (though it is pretty much the only formula in practice), is that by viewing cinema in this manner the viewer can never understand the cinematic philosophy that the actual filmmaker was practicing. From this, something is truly lost.

As the years have gone on and I have gotten progressively more-and-more into embracing the tenets of Pure Cinema (Cinéma Pur); i.e. taking filmmaking to its most elemental core of simply focusing on visually interesting images, movement, and music, I have witnessed how the focus of those who watch my particular brand of cinema (Zen Filmmaking) has not evolved. People are still discussing films I made twenty years ago or more. Why is this? Because, in those films, people find story structure (as minimal as that may be in my films). They find something to talk about. But, in all this talking, again, they have missed the point of what is actually taking place in front of their eyes because they are basing all of their thoughts and discussions upon personal definitions and judgment. This isn't right or wrong—it is simply the way it is. But, by living your life defined by what you have already come to expect, you miss all of the pure and elemental beauty of what is going on in front of you.

For me, filmmaking has always been a spiritual process. Whether my films have been dialogue driven or simply a vision moving across the screen, what I have attempted to do is to harness an elemental image of life and capture it in its essential perfection that existed for only that moment in time. Most people don't get. I understand. That's fine. I am sure that the majority of the people who have watched my films; loving or hating them, have never seen the work of Cinéma Pur filmmakers like Léger, Ray, Richter, Eggeling, Chomette and the list goes on. In fact, if they watched their work they may not even like them as they are so ethereal. But, again, this goes to the elemental nature of cinema and cinema viewing; if you are there expecting something, if you are there judging something, if you are not there in the meditative purity of the moment than your absolute experience is lost—there will be no cinematic satori.

As always in life, let go and be free. See everything as if you are seeing it for the first time and never view anything through the eyes of preconceived judgment. Believe me, if you practice this philosophy, your everything will become better.

Perplexing…
11/Sep/2017 10:26 AM

You know, it has always been immensely perplexing to me how people speak about me, maybe discussing my creations, believing they know what I think, how I think, and why I do what I do. But, they never talk to me. I have had articles written about me: my films or my books without the author ever giving me a phone call. I have had academic dissertations written about Zen Filmmaking by people who never asked me anything. I have had documentaries made about me without the filmmaker ever communicating with me on any level. People have talked about me in books, articles, and on the internet without ever confirming their facts. And film reviews; forget about it… Some of them have been so wrong it is not even funny. But, if they would have just asked me, I could have straightened out any misconception.

Some people love me and have done really positive pieces about me. That's cool! Some have been just the opposite. But, what is missing in all of these equitation is the, *"Me,"* factor. Nobody talks to me. I'm alive! I'm not dead!

Now, I am not saying this is universally the case. A lot of people, since the dawning of the age of the internet, have reached out to me. If they were cool, I was cool. I have had some great discussions via the internet. If they were not cool, then the dialog ended before it ever began. But, more than that, I'm a person; I am approachable. I'm just a guy who does what he does… No better, no worse than anyone else. But, due to all of these previously detailed factors, where people have spoken about me who do not actually know me or understand why I do what I do, people have all of these misconceptions about me. And, some lies have been perpetuated. But, why? The answer is, they have not reached out a hand to know me. I am knowable! Maybe you will like me, maybe I will like you, maybe it will be just the opposite. But, if you don't try you will never know.

And, all this goes to the whole reality of life. Why do you spend your time not knowing? Why do you spend your time guessing and maybe perpetuating a lie? Why do you not go to the source? If you do not go to the source you will never know the truth. Do you want to live your life not knowing the truth?

How Much of What You Say is Wrong?
06/Sep/2017 04:35 PM

I think we have all encounter the know-it-all. ...The person who is always at the forefront of telling people what they think about this or that and presenting their words in a manner as if they were actually the truth. People like this tend to find a lot of followers. Why is that? Because most people don't want to think for themselves. They want to be told how to think and what to think. Thus, the know-it-all provides them with a service—the ability to not have to think for themselves. ...All they have to do is listen and agree.

But, there is a big problem in this entire calculation. That problem is, what a lot of people say is simply flat out not the truth. Though they present their opinions as fact, and maybe they even dig up a few references to make what they are saying seem substantiated. But, if what they say is not true, then it is not true no matter how many misrepresented facts they present in support of their claim.

When I have taught classes at the university level I have encountered this style of behavior quite frequently. Some of these students are very smart or they would not be taking graduate level classes. As they are smart they oftentimes fall prey to their own intellect. Or maybe, they fall prey to their own ego—believing that what they know is what they know and what they believe must be the truth. But, is it?

Certainly, in this tumultuous currently political climate we have here in the United States, you see this all the time with the talking heads on TV. They all are presenting their opinions as if they were facts. And, they present them with such genuineness that it sounds like what they are saying must be the truth. But, when you look at the factual data, what so many of these people are saying is so wrong that it is not even funny. Yet, there they sit in front of the TV camera spreading their gibberish to the world. They are on TV, they must be telling the truth; right?

Are these people liars? Well, not really… They are simply impassioned purveyors of falsity. They believe what they speak but what they believe is not based upon the truth only their fervent opinion.

Remember an opinion or a judgment is never the truth even if one claims that it is. All it can ever be is an opinion and/or a judgment no matter how loudly they scream.

Think about yourself and the way you communicate. Is what you say factual or is it opinion posing as fact? And, where does your knowledge come from? Does it come from the sourcepoint of the truth or are you just lazy and listening to and believing what someone else has to say? Moreover, if you find out you are wrong—if someone explains to you that what you are saying is not actually the truth, do you have the inner strength and/or the morality to correct what you have said and stop repeating it?

Life should be based on truth. Is your life based on the truth?

*   *   *

06/Sep/2017 08:58 AM

How do you un-make a mistake?

* * *

05/Sep/2017 09:52 AM

If you don't believe that you are a sinner does that mean you have not sinned?

If you think that you have not sinned, ask the person you have sinned against what is their opinion of your culpability. Perhaps then you will find the true answer.

How Much of What You Have is Because of Someone Else?
05/Sep/2017 07:19 AM

How much of what you have—what you do and what you have become is because of someone else? And, do you ever think about this fact—do you ever give them thanks?

As we pass through life each of us is taught, influenced, and provided things, both physical and mental, by other people. From what we receive, our life is shaped. This certainly goes to both the positive and the negative elements that we receive but whatever the case, none of us are wholly created by ourselves.

Take a look at your life. How did you get to where you are today?

Most of us come from a defined family. How did your family influence who you are at this moment of your life? In most cases, they paid for your upbringing, put a roof over your head when you were a child, perhaps they paid for you to go to school, and so on. As they are your family, as you do see them and think about them on a regular basis, you commonly can easily define what they did for your life that guided you to whom you have become; maybe you even thank them. But, beyond your immediate family what and whom has guided you to becoming who you are at this moment.

We have each had teachers that have encouraged us and guided us on our path. Through these teachers we have become motivated to become whom we have wanted to become. But, one of the key things to study as you analyze whom you owe what to is, understanding the fact that the teacher you learned from also taught others. What did others do with that knowledge? For example, in my early years, there were a few martial arts instructors who truly helped me on my path. But, they also taught other students. Yet, few of those other students continued their progression and evolution in the martial arts as say I did. So, what was the influence of that teacher on those people? This is the same with myself as a teacher—whether this was in the martial arts, filmmaking, or on other subjects, some of my students have moved into their own, while others did not. Thus, this all comes down to the interpersonal emotional make up of the individual and what they do with what they have learned.

What have you done with what you have learned? Who influenced you to become who you are? And, what do you owe that person?

More than simply the people who have taught and influenced us to be guided in a particular life direction, there are also those people who do material things for us. Maybe they are the person who gave you the job you applied for. From their action you were allowed to make a living. Do you ever think about what you owe them and what their action did to touch your life?

As we pass though our existence most people never think to the subtle elements that came to shape their life. Yes, they may love or hate a person based upon emotions but those are not refined elements, they are simply sensations based upon passions.

Who you actually are and what you have actually become has been shaped by particular people. Some you may know and have studied from personally, while others may be distance in time and in space. But, you did not become who you have become wholly by yourself. You need to realize this. Then you need to look to whom gave you what. I would say that you should thank them from what they gave you but that is a personal choice—a choice that few people choose to make. But, at least you should credit them, in your own mind if nothing else, for their helping you find yourself, in the space and the place, where you live today.

*   *   *

04/Sep/2017 07:50 AM

Just because you don't like somebody does not make them a bad person.

Are you a bad person because somebody does not like you?

* * *
04/Sep/2017 07:46 AM

Making things worse never makes anything better.

*   *   *

03/Sep/2017 07:37 AM

You can't undo what you've already done. Now what?

Do you lie about the fact that you did it?

Do you pretend that you didn't do it?

Do you justify why you think it was okay that you did it?

Or, do you attempt to fix any damage you created by doing it?

Surrender to the Obvious
03/Sep/2017 07:33 AM

Do you go to church? If you do you surrender to the fact that someone knows something more about the greater understanding of the universe than you do and that god should be the elemental focus of your life.

Do you meditate? If you do you surrender to the fact that your mind is not perfect and you need to learn how to calm it, focus it, and control your emotions.

Do you perform Selfless Service? If you do you surrender to the fact that you are not the center of the universe and that by preforming physical acts to make the life of other people better than you are actually doing something to help humanity.

Most people spend most of their life thinking only about themselves: what they want, what then need, what they hope to become, what they like, and what they dislike. Though these people are in the majority, they are not the best example of humanity. In fact, they are just the opposite. They are the best example of selfishness.

Life become more when you become more. Life becomes more when you remove yourself as the center of the equation and look beyond yourself to the larger scheme of reality.

Surrender to the obvious that life is not just about you. Surrender to the fact that there are millions upon millions of people out there, each with needs, feeling, and emotions, who's life would become more is you simply stopped thinking about yourself, got up, and did something to actually helps them.

Surrender to the obvious.

The Power That You Think You Have
02/Sep/2017 07:58 AM

So many people, as they pass through life, strive to hold power. They want to be seen as knowers, doers, the one with the key, the person who is All That. Some people set a conscious course to achieve this level of suchness. They go to medical school, law school, the seminary, they become police officers. Though these people may end up having the credentials, as in all cases in life, it is what you do with what you have the defines you as a human being and what your life will become.

There are others who hold no diploma but, none-the-less, push their ideologies and will in, on, and towards others. They say things, they do things, they force their thoughts and their control onto others. Some even do this with a smile upon their face. But, the reaction to the actions they are unleashing have the same effect. What comes from their mind affects the life of another person or persons whether that person wants to be affected/infected or not.

If what you are doing is helping someone, what you are doing is good. If what you are doing is hurting someone/anyone, what you are doing is bad. It is a very simple life formula, yet so few people adhere to it. All they are driven by is their own desire for power, fame, control, respect, eminence, admiration, and love. Thus, they damage the lives of people. And, this is nothing new, it has been going on forever.

In this world where there are cameras everywhere, where everyone possesses a camera, and even cops are forced to wear body cams, a lot more is documented than what was once brought to light. I used to train a lot of law enforcement professional in the martial arts and the stories they would tell me about some of the things they did was mind blogging. But, they did what they did behind the guise of the badge. I have also watched as people rose to the top of the leap in the entertainment industry, walking all over other people to get there. They lived lavish lifestyles. But, I have also watched as many of these people fell from grace. What was their sin? They hurt people. They didn't care about people. They thought what they were thinking, what they were saying, and what they were doing was more important than what anyone one else was feeling. And, that is just not right.

So, as you walk your pathway through life, keep this in mind: everything that you do sets your own destiny into motion. What you say to others, what you do to others, what you say about others, how you treat others, all has a defining factor upon the ultimate destiny of your life. And though your desire to be revered may cause you to act in an inappropriate, unthinking, and uncaring manner, it is you who will ultimate pay the price for this behavior if you hurt the life of anyone.

The Things That You Own
01/Sep/2017 07:42 AM

Do you ever think about the things that you own?

Looking at the aftermath of the devastation that took place in Texas from Hurricane Harvey, it truly puts a finite perspective onto what people own. As the flood waters have begun receding, in some of the affected communities, you see that the people have returned to their homes to remove all that was destroyed. There are all of these gigantic piles of stuff out in front of the houses. All this stuff that they once possessed, now discarded.

How much of what you own do you really need?

There has been a television series about hoarders on for a number of years now. The storyline is always the same; someone for some reason starts collection and the collection overwhelms them. Why can't these people stop? Can you?

I have known hoarders that have called themselves collectors. The walls of their house were lines with boxes full of CDs, LPs, VHSs, DVDs, books, and comic books. Though very organized, did they need or use any of that stuff?

I have also known hoarders who were so obsessive that if they bought a book they would photocopy it and keep both copies. Why? Just something in their mind that made them do it. Their life and their home became overwhelmed by stuff.

I have watched some people buy a new car but keep the collection of their old cars in their backyard. Why? Some sort of distorted sentimentality, I guess? But, all it equaled was an eyesore.

I have watched as one of my family members piled up all of his stuff in a garage. It was piled floor to ceiling. When it came time to sell the house he tried to go through all the stuff but couldn't and decided the only thing to do was call the guys at Got Junk and they took it all away. Decades of collecting gone. But, why? What did it prove?

Some people even think that the amount of stuff they own defines them as affluent. So, they buy and buy. But, to what end? What does it truly prove?

I have watched people go bankrupt due to the possession they have bough, based upon their belief that they were what they needed. But, all that stuff equals nothing if it hampers your life.

I remember the first time that I truly took note of the level of collecting unnecessary items that some people embrace. I had a close friend that I came up with in Hollywood. He and I truly explored the spiritual path together, laying the foundation for my later years. He decided to move to Santa Cruz with his roommate and his roommate's girlfriend to finish his studies at UC Santa Cruz. He asked and I helped them move. But, the amount of stuff his roommate owned was mindboggling. Usually, in your late teens, early twenties, you don't own that much stuff. But, this guy's stuff filled an entire large U-Haul truck. Crazy... It was not an easy moving experience.

Then, you think about all the people who collect until they die and then someone else, having no care for their possession, gives it all to the thrift shop. Gone...

There are things that we each own that we truly use and/or truly like. There are also things that we own, that though we may not actually use anymore, we believe that they define us as who we are. I know I own several books that fall into that category. But, then there is all this other stuff that we buy because we think we like it, want it, need it, and it then surrounds us. Surrounds us until it is no more or we are no more.

What if you were to die right now. What would happen to all of your stuff?

When you move, this is commonly the time when you discard a lot of that unused stuff because you don't want to go through the labor of moving it. But, there are a lot of people who never move. And, there's a lot of stuff that people refuse to part with for whatever reason. But, all this comes down to the same question, *"Do you ever think about the things that you own?"*

Does your stuff define who you are? And, what if, through an event like Hurricane Harvey, your stuff was no more? Then what? Who are you? What are you?

It is very common as we pass through life that we collect things. Some stuff is a reminder of a time and place in our life. But, do you ever look around your life—the life that you have created for yourself and study what you own, why you own it, what it means to your life, and why do you keep it as a part of your life at all?

It is a common understanding that the less we own, the freer we are, and the less bound to the turmoil of the material world we become. Though pretty much everyone comprehends this understanding, it is embraced by very few people. How about you?

Take a moment right now. Look around your life. Think about the things you own. Define each of them. Why do you own it? What does it mean to your life? What would your life be like without it? Now that you have this definition, what are you going to do about it?

If nothing else this will help you come to a clearer understanding of who you are, what you are, why you are doing what you are doing, and why you own what you own.

*   *   *

30/Aug/2017 03:04 PM

Do you really believe that when you die it will all be explained?

* * *

29/Aug/2017 07:29 AM

When you instigate the actions taken by others you are responsible for those actions.

How Choice Equals Your Everything
29/Aug/2017 07:15 AM

As we pass through our life we each make choices. In many incidences, these choices are something that we have chosen to do in the moment with little forethought. Whether they ultimately turn out to be a good, positive choice or a bad, negative choice, the ramifications from that choice are lived but then we are allowed to move on, leaving our past behind. This is not always the case, however. In some cases, these choices come to define much of the rest of our life. This is certainly the case when someone commits a crime and is caught and legally punished for it. This is also the case when someone meets someone, has a child with them, comes to truly dislike that person, but they are forced to deal with that person, due to the child, for much of the rest of their life.

The previous examples are two of the very obvious ones. There are understandably other actions that people choose to make that binds them to a specific period of their life and a specific person in their life. In many cases, they do this without ever thinking about the larger ramifications of the choice(s) they make on their life and to the life of the person or persons who are affected by the choice that they made. But, whether the action was a conscious choice or not, they bind themselves to that specific choice and/or a specific person. Thus, they become defined by a definable point in their past throughout the rest of their life.

Take a look at your life. Think to the things that define your life. Who are you, what are you? Who are the people around you and why are they there? Now, focus on the things that caused you to become that person. Then, trace this back to the choices you made that caused you to emerge to the point where you find yourself in life. What can you conclude? There is no right or wrong answer, this is simply a prescribed pathway which allows you to see how you have become the person whom you have become.

Once you have a clear perspective of yourself, take a few moments and look to the people whom you've interacted with throughout your life. Now, think to the people you have positively touched as you passed through life. What did you do to make them have that affirmative experience? Next, think about the people whose life you have damaged as you made the choices that you made as you have lived your life. What did you do to hurt them and why did you make that choice?

It is essential to note that the karmic ramification of someone you have hurt are always far stronger than someone you have helped? Why is that? Because pain, (physical, emotional, or otherwise), is long-lasting, especially when you have done nothing to undo the damage. Thus, that person is continually thinking about what you have done and this will forever become a defining factor to your existence in their mind. Thus, the two of you are bound together, via a negative experience, forever.

Think to the people that have been bound to you by the actions you have taken based upon the choices you have made. Define in your mind, the type of relationship that developed between the two of you based upon the choices you have made leading to the actions you have taken. Do you care about the way they feel or how their life has become defined by what you have chosen to do?

For a person with a conscience and a clear awareness of morality they do care. This is what defines them, their relationships, and the choices that they make throughout time. But, there are others out there who do not care. Though you may wish for them to care, you may tell them to care, but again they make their own choices which sets their interactive destiny into motion and if they are a person who does not possess a conscience there is little you or anyone else can do to make them refine and cultivate their mind.

So, what does this leave us with? It leaves us with the fact that not only your life but the life of all those you interact with, as you pass through your life, is defined by the choices you make. It is then further defined based upon the next level of choices you make delineated by the choices you previously made.

What choices will you make today that will define your future? What choices will you make today that will remedy the choices you have made in the past? Your life, your choice.

* * *
29/Aug/2017 07:13 AM

Your life is meant to be remembered. Your dreams are not. Why is that?

* * *
29/Aug/2017 07:13 AM

Your interpretation of another person's life is only your interpretation of another person's life. At best, it is speculation.

The wise person only interprets their own life.

The Knowledge You Possess
27/Aug/2017 03:02 PM

The knowledge you possess defines who you are.

The knowledge you possess defines what you can become.

Though these two declarations may be understood to be proclamations of the obvious, there is a much subtler realm to the fact of how the level of your knowledge defines your life.

What is it that you know? Take a look at all levels of your life. Think about what you believe to be true in terms of your life, your religion, your politics, your friends, your family, and all other realms of knowledge that defines your life. Now ask yourself, *"Why do you know what you know and where did that knowledge come from?"*

For most people they were taught what to believe. Maybe that was in school, maybe that was in church, maybe that information came from family or friends. But, what is to say that any of what you believe is true? All we have to do is to look to how the knowledge of a subject like in the medical sciences has changed vastly over just a couple of decades to understand that knowledge is as fleeting as the time period where it was envisioned. And, this is a concrete science, not something as speculative as say religion or politics.

Another essential question to contemplate is, *"Why do you choose to believe what you believe?"* The fact is, especially in speculative knowledge, a person chooses to believe something. Yes, they may have been taught that fact, they may have heard that fact spoken by another person, but it is only they who decides whether or not to believe it.

Have you ever had the experience of reading a book and you came away with a completely different interpretation of what was being said than say your friend who read the same book? This is just a very small example but think about the larger subjects like the various factions that exists within defined religious groups. Sure, they may all be Christians, Muslims, or Buddhist, they may source their knowledge from the same religious text, but they believe totally different things. How is that possible? That is based in the fact of varying interpretation; in other words, belief.

So, what is knowledge? And, how does knowledge define your life?

Yes, if you have studied a subject and have earned a degree in that subject you may possess the ability to teach that subject. And perhaps, that is the first thing to look for in a person that is proclaiming that what they are saying is, in fact, viable knowledge and not just opinionated judgment. If you want any knowledge to become a viable commodity in your life it must be more than simply belief. It must move past simply the level of personal conviction and transcend into the sphere of a viable, useful medium that becomes a commodity that can actual affect not only your own existence but the life of others, as well.

Far too many people become lost in a space of belief, supposing that it is knowledge. It is not. There is a large difference between belief and knowledge. Belief is something that you know. Knowledge is something that is universally known. Thus, belief is the largest opponent to true knowledge and, as such, it keeps people from becoming all that they could have been.

Do you confuse belief with knowledge? Do your spread your belief as if it were knowledge? If you do, you are doing a disservice to all of humanity. Belief is what has caused all of the problems in the world while knowledge is fact. A fact that can help the universal whole.

Make sure you understand the difference between belief and knowledge. Then, use your knowledge to move your life and the life of everyone else forward.

* * *

27/Aug/2017 07:15 AM

If you are defined by defining others what is the definition of your life?

* * *
25/Aug/2017 06:59 AM

If you would have been awake you wouldn't have had that nightmare.

* * *
24/Aug/2017 08:59 AM

What contribution have you made to the evolution of culture?

   * * *
24/Aug/2017 08:57 AM

People who are intrinsically angry always look for something to be angry about.

What is the root source of your anger?

You may blame someone outside of yourself for making you angry but it is you who chooses to embrace that negative emotion.

* * *

23/Aug/2017 07:54 AM

"It's my fault."

How often do you acknowledge this fact?

*   *   *
23/Aug/2017 07:51 AM

How quickly did you let go of your dream?

For the Last Time
23/Aug/2017 07:40 AM

Is there a place that you really like to go or something that you really like to do? Maybe there is this one restaurant that you really enjoy eating at. Now, think about this, what if you were in the last stage of your life, would you have the chance to eat at that restaurant or go to that place one last time and what would that mean to your overall life experience?

As we are living beings we will, one day, live no more. Most people avoid this fact until they are in the final stage of their life. Then, when they are pushed up against the wall of death, they remember all of the things that they once loved and this memory causes them to desire to experience them one more time. In some cases, these dreams are small, so experiencing them is not out of the question. In other cases, these dreams exist thousands of miles away or maybe, that place remembered, no longer exists; then what? How can that moment of happiness or enjoyment be relived?

There is the place in all of us where when we find that special something that touches our inner being and we truly bond with it. Some of these experiences are quite fleeting. In other cases, they are defined by whom we were with or what our state of mind was during that particular point in our life. When and if we ever go back, the experience may be totally different. Yet, in that one moment of time, that one experience of fullness is etched into our being so we wish to relive it.

Have you ever really loved a restaurant but when you go back to it, some time later, everything has changed? Maybe the staff, the food, or the clientele has completely changed and you are left wondering what you ever liked about that place.

As one of the definitive elements of life is that we do not live forever, this too is the definitive element of places.

Things change. Moreover, what you felt at one point in your existence is defined by that time period of your existence. What you were then, you may not be now.

It is for this reason that looking to the past to regain a past experience and/or feeling virtually never plays out the way you would have it do so in your mind. Nothing in this life ever stays the same. Just as no two experiences, in one specific place, are ever the same.

So, what does this tell us? It reminds us to love any experience we live while it is happening. Because maybe it will never happen again. It also tells us to keep our eyes on what is in front of us as opposed to being locked into a place of the past.

The past is gone. Hopefully you had some great experiences back there, back when. But, here is all you have. Going back is at best an attempt to cast your mind into a realm of something that can never be as good as it was remember.

* * *
22/Aug/2017 08:54 AM

What did you do to create the moment you are living right now?

Do Onto Others
22/Aug/2017 07:42 AM

Do you ever contemplate the biblical quote: Luke 6:31, *"Do onto others as you would have the do onto you?"* I think we have all heard this statement for most of our lives but how many of us ever think about it? But, maybe we should.

The things you do in life have the potential to affect your everything. What you do to other people not only has the potential to affect the life of the person you are doing it to but your life as well as there are always repercussion to all of your actions, be they positive or negative.

Many people dismiss the concept of, doing onto to others. Think about it, do you? Do you only think about yourself? Do you only think about how what you are doing will affect your existence? Moreover, do you ever take the time to watch and witness what other people are doing and how they are doing what they are doing to other people? If you watch and study this behavior it will give you a very clear insight into the mind of that person—who they are, how they think about themselves, how they treat others and, from this observation, you can chart how they will ultimately treat you.

Doing onto others is not only based upon the doing of big things. It begins at the very small level; as small things are what set the big things into motion. Think about the smallest thing you have done for a person: whether it was removing a piece of lint from their clothing, pouring them a cup of coffee or getting them a beer. All actions have extended reactions. What occurred because of what you did? If you say, *"Nothing,"* you are wrong, you are not looking to the extended ramifications of your actions.

Now, think about the big things you have done that have affected the life of another person. First of all, would you have wanted that done to you? Would you have wanted to encounter the consequences of that actions? At this point contemplate, what did your doing do to your life? Did what you did make your existence a more positive space or did it cause you to encounter turmoil?

The human race is very selfish breed. But, the human race is also a very thinking breed. We can choose to make the right choice and do the right thing. How often do you do that? How often do you think about the other person first? How often do you, do onto others as you would have the do onto you?

Art and the Forgotten Remembered
21/Aug/2017 08:54 AM

There has been a certain romance attached to writers who did not become famous until after their death. People like H.P. Lovecraft, Edgar Allen Poe, or even Henry David Thoreau, though they each had some of their work published while they were alive, they mostly lived in poverty and died unknown—never knowing the audience their work would eventually find. It was the people who read them after their passing that understood their work and sent them in the direction notoriety. Biographies have been written, discussions have been had, movies have been made about their life, and courses have been taught all based upon the writing of authors such as this. But, what about the writers that have been completely forgotten? Maybe they were published, maybe they were not, but no matter their publishing status, no one remembers their name—no one studies their work. Do we, can we ever think about the contributions of those writers? And, was their vision and/or contribution any the less than that of those that became known?

In many ways, there is something very disingenuous about honoring someone who was shunned during their life but loved after their death. Certainly, whether one found an audience before or after their death does not change the contribution they made. But, what ultimately brought them to the level where their works could be read by the masses, after they died, as opposed to when they were still alive, raises the question of why?

We can also look to the life of someone like Vivian Maier. She was a woman who made her living as a nanny but spent her free time taking beautiful photographs of predominately the urban landscape. In her life, she found no fame in her art. But, upon her passing in 2009, exhibitions began to be held; initially motivated, in no small part, due to the fact that she could no longer afford the rent on her storage unit that held thousands of her negatives and thus it was auctioned off. Think about the TV show, Storage Wars. (Does anyone ever think about the reason those units are being auctioned off as they watch that show?) In any case, a vast amount of her work was brought to the daylight but it was too late. She died two years later before they could figure out who she was.

This whole subject really brings us to the essence of art. Particularly in this day and age of the internet where some people are very loud. But, does loudness mean that they possess the true essence of art or does it simply mean that they scream louder than the true artist? And, this is the thing, when someone is in the forefront of modern consciousness, whether they are alive or dead, they are the one that people think about and perhaps even idolize. But, does being in that position elementally provide them with a voice worth hearing? What about the person out there in the abyss who creates true art but is never seen or heard? Is their art any the less? Or, is it actually a purer portrayal of art for they were silent in the quintessence of its creation?

You can scream loud and people will hear you. But, does screaming loud make you an artist or does it simply make you loud? You can be silence and own the essence of true art, but if you create art that no one ever sees, will you ever be known as an artist?

This is a complex question and a motivation for you to seek out true art wherever you can find it. Known or not, sometimes the unknown leads you to the true soul of art and the artist.

Regretful Actions
19/Aug/2017 07:46 AM

As we pass through life, each of us performs actions that we later regret. In some cases, these actions hurt other people and though, at the time, we may have thought that we were doing the right the thing, through further self-examination we realized that what we did was wrong, we hurt someone or something, and we regret it.

Most of us have a conscience. Though we may do something, spurred on by whatever motivation, when we later are either told we did something wrong or we come to realize it on our own, we regret our actions and attempt to repair any damage we created.

Not everyone is like this, however. Some people do not care who or what they injure. They behave in this manner due to a combination of factors: ego, denial, insecurity, support of other people, and various other reasons. But, for the person who behaves in this manner, they walk a life trek of creating damage while existing in a state of self-imposed justifications. Thus, if you look back through their life it is easy to see that they have injured many people and this is never a good thing.

Generally, when we do something that we later regret, it is done to a person. The reason we hurt other people is commonly based upon lack of awareness, selfishness, or a lack of empathy. We feel something and we do it. Many of these actions are lived in the moment. Our emotions are elevated so we act out. From this, a lot of life damage can be instigated.

All you have to do is watch a live action television show like COPS or Live PD and you will see how the interactions of two people, based upon emotions, can elevate to create interpersonal havoc.

This is case with abusive relationships, as well. There is commonly one person instigating either the psychological or the physical abuse. But, the question that is rarely asked is, why are they doing it? In some cases, it was due to that person growing up in a very abusive environment and, thus, that type of behavior is all that they know. In other cases, the person who is performing the abuse blames the person they are abusing for forcing them into a relationship that they did not want to be a part of. As we can see, there are two actors and two points of view. The problem with this equation is, however, the people who exist in these relationships are commonly not aware enough to see what is actually going on. Thus, a lot of bad actions can be performed when the best thing that could have happened is that the one person who desires the relationship should have simply walked away, thereby freeing the both of them from further emotional and physical pain, leading to blame and regret.

Do the people who exist in these relationship feel regret based upon their interrelationship actions? I imagine some do and some do not.

Now, this relationship basic goes to business relationships, as well. Commonly, there is one person in a position of control in any business dealings. From this, comes the condition of master and servant. One person works for the other person and they must do what is asked of them if they wish to remain employed. The very big difference between the personal and the work relationship is that in the situation of employment, people are commonly there because they need to make a living to support themselves and their family. Thus, simply walking away is not necessarily all that easy.

I am sure we have all heard about people that were in less than ideal and even abusive relationship brought on by the actions of their employer—some of us have even been in those situations. Now, we can all hope and wish that people exist based upon a space of refined caring and consciousness but unfortunately this is not the case in life. Many people, especially when they are in a position of power, operate from an ego driven mindset. This mindset arises from many factors of causation but not the least of which is one that it is based upon the cheering on of those who surround that person, whether this be other employees, friends, family, or whomever.

I remember an ideal example of this, *"Cheered on mentality,"* that I witnessed many years ago. I was driving home in the early AM hours of the morning. I noticed this group of people arguing in the parking lot of a 711. One guy was behind the wheel of a car and he apparently had almost hit a guy who was walking as he was backing out of a parking space. This caused an argument. The guy who was almost hit was yelling. The friends of the guy driving the car got out and are taunting the guy who was walking who, at this point, would not get out of the way of the car. The friends are all yelling, *"Hit him! Hit him!"* Eventually, the guy driving the car, motivated by the cheering of his friends, steps on the gas and plows into the guy. Whatever became of any of those people, I do not know. But, this is an obvious example of what can motive a person to perform a really bad deed. And, it is smothering that you really need to think about when your friends are telling you to do anything that has the potential to hurt anyone.

At the heart of a living a good life is possessing a conscience. We all make mistakes but it is what we do after we make those mistakes that defines us as a human being. What is a mistake that should be regretted? Anything that hurts anyone for any reason.

Ask yourself, have you hurt someone? Has someone told you that you hurt someone or something? After you were told, what did you do? Did you care? You want a definition of your life and what it will ultimately equal, the response to those question will provide you with an answer.

As previously detailed, there may be fault and blame that goes in many directions in any interpersonal interaction that turns out badly. But, no matter who is the instigator or the culprit, it is what each person who is involved in that interaction does with the experience that sets the stage for the rest of their life.

Some people feel no regret and that is sad. Other people deny fault, that is also sad. In fact, I have watched some people as they came up against the wall of death apologizing to people for their bad deeds. I have also literately witnessed one person, who did a lot of bad things, especially to his family, not seek forgiveness at any level. He never said he was sorry. Instead, all he did was to ask the doctor if he could give him a shot to kill him. He just wanted to get off of the bus.

What you do creates who you are. What you do after the fact of doing something defines you as a human being. Do you blame you or do you constantly try to shift the blame outwards onto someone else? If you instigated anything, you are to blame. If you took part in anything, you are to blame.

Taking the blame is one of the highest levels of human consciousness as is shows you care more about someone else than you care about yourself. Who do you care about? The more people you care about, the more forgiveness you seek, the more you and your life becomes a positive example to others.

Speaking Your Mind Verse Mindful Speaking
18/Aug/2017 08:01 AM

One of the primary tenets of Buddhism is *Right Speech.* It is an essential part of *The Eightfold Path.*

In the modern world, especially in the Free World, people have the belief that they can say whatever it is they want to say with impunity. Perhaps this is true from a governmental perspective but is what is allowed by society the only true definition of human consciousness? No. Just because you think something, that does not make it true. Just because you are allowed to say whatever it is you want to say, that does not make it right. On the path of rising human consciousness the individual should make a cognizant decision to formulate their speech from a more profound perspective then simply letting their thought and beliefs run away with their thinking mind, thereby creating the words they are speaking. That is what sets the person walking the spiritual path in a different direction than the average person; they consciously formulate every aspect of what they do and what they say in order to leave the least amount of impactful devastation in their wake.

Right Speech is based initially upon the Buddhist concept of *Right Thought.* For, where do your words arise from? They are instigated by what you think. But, why do you think what you think? This goes to the source of whom you associate with. Thus, the Buddhist understanding of *Right Association* is brought into play. Whom you associate with equals what you think, equals what you say.

As sentient beings, we all feel we are whole and compete onto ourselves. This is also the sourcepoint for where the human ego comes into play. As we are whole and complete beings, many feel that gives them the right to do and say whatever it is they want. But, again, this goes back to the sourcepoint for personal thought. Why do you choose to think what you think? What was your inspiration? Why do you feel you have the right to spread what you think out to the world via your words? What made you believe that it was acceptable to do that?

At the heart of all rising human consciousness is the person who chooses to take control over themselves. They do this realizing that they are not the All Powerful, All Knowing Being that the ego has allowed many to embrace. They understand that they are simply a cog in the wheel and, as such, what they do has an ever-rippling effect onto the rest of world. From this understanding, they choose to take control over their mind and the actions unleashed by their thoughts so that the world becomes a better, less traumatized place. Thus, they choose mindful speaking over speaking their mind.

Where do you place yourself in the spectrum of the existence that you find yourself currently living? Do you feel that you have the God-given-right to expound your beliefs to all those who will listen? If you do believe this, where did that belief arise? And, do you not believe that everything you say possesses an impact on the lives of not only those you speak about but those who listen to your words? Do you not believe that you are creating your own karma by saying what you are saying?

It takes a strong person to put their ego in check. It takes a strong person to not be dominated by what they think and what they believe. It takes a strong person to understand that mindful words are the sourcepoint for making the world a better place as opposed to making it a more damaged place on both the interpersonal and universal level.

Can you be strong enough to choose *Right Speech?* This is a question that you can only answer yourself. But, be advised, your words equal your karma and your words equal your destiny. What kind of life do you want to live? What kind of impact do you wish to invoke?

* * *

18/Aug/2017 07:20 AM

When you judge the impact you are having on the life of another person it is always evaluated from the position of you.

* * *
17/Aug/2017 06:56 PM

When what you do affects the life of somebody else, your karma is created. If what you are doing is hurting anyone, what do you think will be the result?

*   *   *

17/Aug/2017 05:03 PM

If you think you've paid your karma for some action that you performed, that generally means that you haven't.

* * *

17/Aug/2017 01:16 PM

Is it okay to lie to a liar?

Looking Without Seeing
17/Aug/2017 07:00 AM

How much of what you see as you pass through your day do you actual look at—do you actually study?

Life is filled with unique elements everywhere you look. But, how often do you actually take the time to take a look? For most of us, we simply pass through our day, expecting what we expect, knowing what we have seen, but we never take a moment to actually see.

Right now, take a minute. Look around yourself. Find something and focus on it. No matter how many times you have seen it before, take this moment and study it. Look at all of the unique details it visually has to offer. Think about what it took to create it. Study it as if you have never seen it before.

The problem for most people is that they have seen what they have seen so many times that they do not even think about the plethora of visual depth that it holds. From this, so much of life passes by without a thought as nothing is appreciated.

When you look to the sky, every minute of every day, its visual-scape is changing. Do you ever think about that? Do you ever take the time to watch those changes unfold? This is the same with the fields, the ocean, the desert, or even the city streets. There are millions upon millions of things going on and changes taking place. There is life and visual stimuli everywhere but they are missed because nobody take the time to take a look.

If you want your life to mean something more. If you want to understand life, nature, and the universe from a more profound level. If you want to understand the art of existence all you have to do is open your eyes. Remember this and cause yourself to do it wherever you find yourself. Your life will become so much more.

* * *

16/Aug/2017 12:52 PM

Earlier today I was doing what you do in L.A.; namely driving between one place and the other. I was listening to NPR and within about an hour I heard two interesting statements that pretty much speak for themselves:

If you know better, you should do better.

Why bother it if it don't bother you.

He's Written Too Many Books, Just Like Me
16/Aug/2017 08:49 AM

In the late 1970s and into the early 1980s, the great East Indian Sage, Bhagwan Shree Rajneesh, used to produce an enormous amount of books. Having spent some time with him in India I can definitely say that he was on the cusp of a spiritual revolution. His approach to turning the tenets of traditional Hinduism and mysticism upside down was truly transformative. But, it was one of those things that you had to be there, you had to meet him there and then, or you just would not understand.

His mistake, if you want to call it that, was that he came to the United States and located his ashram in a less than forward thinking community. But, this being said, he did have a message. A message that was overrun by the press and the upheaval over his Rolls Royce driven lifestyle. Some people just didn't get it… But, you can find out all about his life and lifestyle online if you want to.

Anyway… Back in that era, I was an undergraduate at Cal State Northridge, teaching the martial arts on a daily basis. I had severed my ties with the Integral Yoga Institute and I was no longer the guy, dressed in yogi garb, collecting the $2.00 at the door for the Sufi Dances every Tuesday night. What Rajneesh had to say, via the written word, helped keep me focused on spirituality. Mostly, what he meant to me was that he provided a look at traditional spirituality in a new and revolutionary way as this was the path I also followed.

I was living in this apartment, not far my university campus, and I remember the boxes full of his beautifully designed hardcover books I would receive—ordered from his ashram. Whenever there were new ones being published, I would get them.

As I have long stated, I was a terrible student with my mind far more focused on other realms of reality than my school work. Instead of reading my textbooks, I remember immediately reading each of the Rajneesh books that arrived, cover-to-cover. They provided me with an ongoing source of inspiration into the abstract realms of spiritual which came to be the focus of my life.

Now, I know... I know... I too have written a lot of a lot of... Some would say way too much. I get it! Like I joking say in the title for this piece, *"He's Written Too Many Books, Just Like Me."* But, just like Rajneesh, if you don't like what I write, you don't have to read it. The difference between Rajneesh and myself is that I actually type everything I write. For him, his books were all based on his lectures being transcribed. I think that must be a far easier way to write a book.

Later in his life, when he had basically been kicked out of the U.S., he asked to be called, Osho. But, when I knew him this was not the name he used so I will continue to use Rajneesh. Anyway, during his lectures, which became his books, he spoke from a very off-the-cuff perspective. He said what he was thinking at the time and then he may change his mind, and say the complete opposite, a moment later. To me, that was true spirituality—pure Zen. Because, isn't the truth of spirituality that it is what is lived in the now—what is experienced right here in this moment?

All this being said, the point of this essay is twofold: First of all, we all should find our inspiration where we can find it. As it is really easy to lose our course in life if we do not possess a means to keep it focused. Thus, whatever it is that you truly ARE in life, develop a method to keep that the focus of your life. Don't lose it! If it means reading books, like I did, going to lectures, yoga classes, martial art classes, church, or the movies, don't let yourself loose what and who you know you are. Find a way to maintain your focus.

The second point is, once upon a time, there were Rajneesh books everywhere. Virtually every bookstore you went into you could find one. Now, except for a few remaining mass-market paperbacks and the occasional one being labeled as, *"Collectable,"* and selling for way too much money on eBay, they are all gone. Gone to where? What happened to them as there were so many that were produced? I guess, just like I have witness with so many people in the world of spirituality and the martial arts throughout my life, a once very well-known individual, who truly made a contribution, has all but been forgotten. Remembered only by those whose lives they touched. So, what does this tell us? I guess it means that we are all only as temporary as the people who remember us. Good or bad, that is the definition of life.

*   *   *
16/Aug/2017 07:49 AM

Is your life defined by what you said or by what you did?

* * *
16/Aug/2017 07:48 AM

As long as you are thinking or saying something negative about someone else you are not doing anything positive with your own life.

In Service to Society
15/Aug/2017 07:55 AM

How much of your time do you spend thinking about what you can consciously do for others?

Very few people, as they pass through life, ever think about what they can do for society. There are very few people who make any kind of contribution whatsoever to the life that surrounds them. They may work hard and perhaps even achieve a high standard of living for their family and themselves but they never even consciously look beyond themselves and question what they can do for the greater whole.

There are certain people who make noticeable contributions to society. The doctors, the police officers, the firemen, and the teachers. These contributions are self-evident because without these people, society would be in chaos.

Though there are these obvious contributors, there are numerous other layers of people who make a contribution but what they give is far less definable. Mostly, at this level, it is people who do something to make a living or to make themselves famous but they are claiming, at least in their own mind, that they are providing a service to the greater whole. But, are they? If the individual persona is involved, if the individual is on the stage saying, *"Hey, look at me,"* is that a contribution at all or is it just a state of egotism? And, how many of these people have hurt the lives of other people while they climbed to their pulpit, thereby erasing any possible good they have done in the first place?

Have you ever gone out of your way; put yourself, your ego, and your own desires aside, and just given? Have you ever done something, that maybe you didn't even want to do, but the doing of it truly helped someone else? If you have had this experience you will understand that it is very rewarding. And yes, though you may have received a positive emotional response when the doing is completed, you have actually done something that formally helped someone. Their life is better. Thus, society is better. Thus, everything, everywhere is just a little bit better.

Can you put yourself away and actual help? Can you make a contribution to society? If you can, not only do you become better, not only are your better remember throughout time, but that one person that you truly helped will never forget you because you provided a service that changed their life.

How much of your time do you spend thinking about what you can consciously do for others?

* * *

14/Aug/2017 03:53 PM

All negative behavior comes from a place of unanswered pain.

* * *

14/Aug/2017 03:04 PM

Think how many people are praying to god, asking for something, right at this moment.

* * *
13/Aug/2017 07:24 AM

How many of the stories that you tell are one hundred percent true?

How many of the stories that you tell are not influenced by your individual perception or how you wished a situation would have played out?

How many of the stories that you hear, told to you by others, are one hundred present true?

How many of the stories that you hear are actual fact and not influenced by an individual's perception or how a person wished that situation would have turned out?

What does this leave us with? A reality based upon factual inaccuracy.

Look to the Family
12/Aug/2017 08:14 AM

There are times in life when you meet somebody and though on the surface they may blend effortlessly into society there is something that, at certain times, takes them off in a completely different direction. This shift in personality is usually heralded by a radical state of mind. Maybe it is intense rudeness, anger, violence, or even exaggerated compassion. Though you may believe you know this person, when these episodes happen, you cannot help but wonder where did this emotion and/or exaggerated reaction come from. If the answer is not obviously, there is always one place to explore; look to the family.

Each person is born with a unique personality. Though they are a unique individual onto themselves, this personality is then shaped by the society they are born into and more demonstratively by their family. For it is at the family level that, from the earliest memories forward, an individual learns how to behave. From this, their actions and reactions to life events are shaped.

In many cases, if you have the ability to know a person and then meet and interact with their family, you will see how the person you know exhibits many of the same traits as their parents and siblings. Though, almost universally, a person will deny this factor as people long to be whole and complete entities onto themselves. And, in many cases, they may not even like their parents so they do not want to appear to be defined by them. But, from the outside looking in, it is commonly much easier to see the correlations than when a person is locked into a specific skin.

Some people are raised in very focused and supportive environment. Though it is almost impossible to get through childhood and adolescences without encountering some conflict with your parents, some people, due to their family upbringing, emerge as very well-formed individuals. Commonly, this is not the case, however. Many people, due to an untold number of factors, comes from families that were not an ideal breeding ground for a healthy and radiant life. It is from within these environments that a person is subtlety taught the ways to behave that have the potential to cause them to react in a less than civilized and enlightened manner as they pass through their life.

It is very hard to find a person who does not wish to be happy, successful, and fulfilled in their life. Virtually everyone understands that the way to achieve this is to do good things that make other people happy while damaging or hurting no one in the process. Yet, when we look around ourselves we see selfish, uncaring, anger driven actions taking place all the time. Where was the mindset born that causes people to behave in this negative manner? Again, look to the family.

When we are forced to encounter a person behaving in an unexpected, exaggerated, or negative manner, it can be quite shocking. For generally, we never see it coming. We are just impacted with it and then left to deal with its reverberations. Though many people who reactively behave in this manner will attempt to attach all types of excuses to their behavior—some may even be sorry in the aftermath. But, that never takes away what was done. This negative doing can be small or it may be large but all that anyone is left with is what one person did that left others questioning why.

With all this being said, there is one elemental component to this equation. That component is, the person themselves. Though we can each reach out and find excuses for our behavior when we have done something that is deemed as wrong—something that has hurt someone or something, the ultimately reality is that there is always only one person to blame. The person who performed the action. That one person did something by choice or by instinct and that something hurt someone or something else. The ultimately answer that each person must master, in their own way, is to learn how to take control over their own emotions and never let them be in control.

Wherever negatively expressed emotions may arise from: self, society, family, or otherwise, it is always only the one person who expresses them. Be more than your out of control emotions no matter where you learned them from.

* * *

12/Aug/2017 08:13 AM

What have you given anyone lately without receiving something in return?

Blaming the Other Person
11/Aug/2017 08:52 AM

Whenever there is an issue between two people there is one person who set that issue into motion. There is one person who did something and from that something conflict was created.

How often have you witnessed when the one person who set that one thing into motion lies, denies, and tries to shift any blame of creating the situation onto the other person. *"It was their fault, not mine!"*

Is reacting to something bad that a person did to you a negative thing? No, not necessarily. Is lying and attempting to deflect responsibly in an undesirable situation you created a negative thing? Yes. But, think about how often this goes on. Do you do it? Do you rally people to your defense even though it was you who initially did that something that set the everything into motion?

This is how large-scale conflicts are created by small events. Somebody does something that hurts someone in some way, they then justify or deny their responsibility in the action, and instead of taking responsibility and perhaps apologizing they rally people to their cause. Then, the other person rallies people to their cause and, thus, a war is born. A war based on a small thing that one person did but refuses to own their responsibility in its creation.

We all make mistakes in life. We all do things that unintentionally hurt someone else. Think how much better the world would be if we all simply owned our actions, apologized, and try to repair any damage we created instead of seeking a reason to blame the other person who was hurt by what we instigated.

Do you ever say you're sorry?

How You Earn Your Keep
11/Aug/2017 08:11 AM

There is this strange belief in the modern world that it does not matter how you earn your money as long as you do earn your money. This concept has led to all kinds of people doing all kinds of bad things. The people who operate from this mindset never think about the consequences they are unleashing on the life of other people as long as they are getting their bankroll and living as large as possible.

Certainly, in popular culture, the person who sells drugs on the street has been glorified. This is especially the case when that person rises from their unlawful beginnings and becomes a sport or a hip hop star. But, does their rising above what they used to do change the fact of all of the people's lives they damaged?

In the realms of the sale of drugs, I have known people that actually believe they are providing a service. People want to get high, right? People need to step away from the day-to-day grind, right? But, at what cost? Think of all the lives that have been ruined due to the use of drugs.

The sale of illegal drugs is illegal. I have known people that have been sent to prison for following this course of making their living. Though they were very bitter about what became of the life, they were the one who choose to do something that was and is deemed, *"Illegal,"* so who was ultimately to blame? So yes, in some cases, they were taken to task for hurting the lives of other people but that does not change the damage they unleashed nor does it repair what happened to the people who ingested the drugs they sold—all based on their wanting to make money.

Though the sale of drugs is an obvious example of one of the things that people do to make money in a less than acceptable manner, there are all kinds of other things that people do while never looking to the larger consequences of their actions. As we all know people abscond with all kinds of commodities on the internet to make money off of the vision, creativity, labor, and finances of other people. Do they care? No. If they did, they wouldn't do it. In fact, if you present them with the fact that they are stealing someone's something to make their money, they will fight you tooth and nail in an attempt to make themselves seem right and justified. But, are they right? No. If you take anything from anybody for any reason that is wrong. It is as simple as that. Yet, think how many people play into this society of internet theft and partake of the products these people have stolen. Are these people ever caught and punished? Rarely.

There are lot of people who live in the world of the various realms of creativity and find a way to get money to maintain their lifestyle from the labor of other people. As many people wish they could be in one of the creative fields, especially the film business, many a less than scrupulous individual has gone to these folks with money, asked them for it, promising them the world of return, and then walked away living a good lifestyle based upon someone else's finances.

There is the other side of the issues, in the creative fields, where people like distributors and publishers take the creative work of others, promising them fame and riches, make a lot of money off of those creations and never share any of the money or accolades with the actual creator of the work. Though I have watched as a few of these people who walk this path of financing their life with other people's money and creativity has been left bankrupt, many maintain their high level of existence throughout their life. They do this while not caring about what they are doing to the life of other people.

This brings us to the heart of this problem of financial existence. As long as a person is making their cash, they do not care about who they are hurting or what negativity they are unleashing to the world as a whole. If they did—if they were conscious people, they would not be doing what they were doing in the first place. But, they are not.

So, what does this leave us with? It leaves us with the simple reality that most people don't care unless they are forced to care. They may pretend that they are providing a service but if that service is based upon taking anything from someone else or damaging the life or anybody, it is no service at all.

Ask yourself, *"Do you care?"* Do you care about what you are ingesting or who you are taking from? Or, do you simply make excuses for your actions? *"I don't have much money." "I'm a poor student." "I'm a struggling artist." "I need to feed my kids." "I have a drug problem so I need money to stay high."* Whatever the justification, that is all that it is, an excuse. If you make your money by stealing, if you make your money by doing things that hurt the life of other people, all you are creating is a world of hurt. No matter what your justification, if what you are doing to make your living hurts anyone it will eventually hurt you.

Think about what you do to pay your rent. Care about what you do.

*   *   *
10/Aug/2017 12:52 PM

Is the injustice you see true injustice or is it simply based upon the perspective of what you want to be right?

                    *   *   *

10/Aug/2017 12:51 PM

If you were to stop thinking about yourself:
       what you want,
       what you need;
what would you think about?

* * *
10/Aug/2017 08:58 AM

If what you are doing is hurting anyone what you are doing is wrong.

But, here is the problem with this equation:

When you look to what you are doing and what you have done, do you think about what someone else has done to you or do you think about what you have done to them?

The righteous person always tries to undo and repair the damage they created before they ever look to what any other person has instigated. Because if you don't, the damages do nothing but multiply.

Care enough to fix what you've broken first.

What Happens When You Leave?
10/Aug/2017 08:38 AM

I was recently thinking back to my days with Swami Satchidananda and the Integral Yoga Institute. I was very-very involved. It was a different point in history and I believe that this is the thing that many people (who are younger) do not really have the perspective to understand. It was the 1970s and spirituality was everywhere. People really cared about rising consciousness, doing the right thing, making the planet a better place, and helping those in need. Many, like myself, found a home in a spiritual group and this became our focus. The people of the Integral Yoga Institute truly became my extended family.

Throughout my years at Hollywood High School, my focus was far more on this other element of my life than going to school. Whereas most young people, as they pass through their high school years, are focused on the reality of the school atmosphere and what it means to them, this was not the case for me. I was there but I was not there. In fact, in many ways, I am very surprised that I stayed in school at all instead of simply following the dedicated spiritual path. Certainly, as my later years came upon me I am so glad that I did graduate but back then, it really didn't matter. It didn't matter so much that I didn't even take my senior picture which is why you will not see me in the 1976 Hollywood High School yearbook. ☺

For me, I was also able to serve a purpose at the Integral Yoga Institute. I became Swami Satchidanand's soundman. From that, I truly felt I was making a contribution to the greater whole of this man's life and his message. I wonder whatever happened to all of those tapes of his talks and lectures that I recorded on reel-to-reel and cassette tape?

The problem with any group, however, is there are those people who are put in a position of authority. Some of them are the nicest people and do their job in a friendly, egoless manner. This is not always the case, however. Some come at it with the, *"I am the boss,"* attitude. As my years progressed with the IYI, I witnessed as a number of egos come into play. I also saw how this became the downfall of the group in places like Los Angeles and Santa Barbara, where Swami Satchidananda had a beautiful house overlooking the coastline in nearby Montecito.

From my perspective, the entire point of following the spiritual path is to become as egoless as possible and as caring as possible. Though selfless service, (karma yoga), was at the root of this organization, many of the people came at this ideology with less than a highly developed and pure mindset. They were not ready to be handed the power, yet they were. These power-trippers are what caused a lot of people, including myself, to eventually leave the group. I didn't leave Swami Satchidananda, I left the group.

But, what happens then? What happens when you are no longer a part of what was once one of the elemental parts of your life? In many ways, this situation happens to many of us. We were once a part of the greater whole—we really felt we were on a mission with our compatriots. But then, something occurs, and our mission is over. We are out there in the alone. What do we do then?

This is different for each person. For me, at the time, I would go and spend time with the various others Eastern spiritual teachers that passed through L.A. I also refocused my attention on the martial arts. But, never being far from the Eastern mindset of spirituality, this drive also eventually led me to India. But, it was there, that I truly came to realize that you can't go and GET spirituality, it must come from within.

I think that is probably the answer for anyone who is out there feeling lost—feeling alone. …Maybe you once had something like a person or a group and you no longer possess it. From this, many keep looking out there to find a replacement. But, there is none. At best, all there can be is you coming into your own, charting your own path that is not dominated by anyone else, (power-tripper or not), and simply you are creating your own reality that is defined by the way you perceive the world.

For those of us who came of age at a time when caring, giving, and spirituality mattered, and for those of us who focused our lives upon these ideologies, we will always possess an undeniable focus for our lives. But, caring, giving, and spirituality is not wholly defined by a specific period of history. It is everywhere if you care enough to open your mind and your heart and give instead of take.

So, wherever you find yourself in life—a part of a group or a part of the greater whole or not, this can be the root of your reality. Get out there and help. Get out there and give. Get out there and care. And, this can begin in the smallest most interpersonal way onto the greatest arena. From this, not only will you find a new wholeness in your life but the entire world becomes just a little bit better.

Agenda
09/Aug/2017 08:47 AM

It is very difficult to interact with most people from a place of consciousness. This is because of the fact that virtually everyone has their own agenda. They never come to a relationship without some form of preconceived notion and/or desire. They see you, they think they know you, they think they know what they want from you, and they set about on a course to obtain it. This is why there is so much interpersonal chaos and pain in the world because people form their definitions of another person based upon what they want from that other person. They may love the person, they may hate the person, they may want something from the person: money, sex, fame, notoriety, position, but what they never do is enter into interaction with that person from a space of spiritual understanding—allowing them to be whole and whom they are; whole and complete onto themselves. Instead, each person wants the other person to be the way they have them defined in their own mind. But, are they? Is another person ever what you expected them to be?

On the other side of the issue, people also form their personas based upon what other people desire. They try to become what someone else wants them to be. Again, this is based upon agenda—they want something from that other person so they strive to be what that other person wants them to be. From this, comes a world of people who base their entire existence upon speculated suchness—upon how they define others and how others define them. Thereby, much of this world is populated by people who are not true onto themselves but are either pretending to be something they are not or are defined by others to be something they are not.

From a spiritual and even psychological perspective this is a very shallow place to live your life from. But, this being said, how many people do it? Do you? Do you define others? Do you allow yourself to be shaped by others? When you interact with people do you pretend to be something you are not so they will like you? And, how do you behave when someone thinks that they know who you are—defines you as a something, but they are totally wrong? Do you play along with the game or do you emphatically state that you are not who they claim that you are?

Life is complex. Very few people care enough about the subtitles of every-rising consciousness to even give it a second thought. They simply exist in a place of believing they are right and, thus, they project that, "*Rightness,*" to the world. But, are they right at all?

The very term, "*Life,*" is defined by what is living. From living we each are given the opportunity to be who and what we are. Most, however, lose this opportunity and become something that is defined by others. Thus, there is very little actual interactive consciousness exhibited between people as they move through life. They simply embrace a false definition of self.

Are you who you are? Or, do you pretend? Do you allow others to be who they are? Or, do you define them in your own mind before they have the opportunity to present themselves as a true and whole human being and then do you project what you believe them to be to the world?

Life is what you make of it. What are you making of it? Do you embrace the wholeness of who you are? Do you allow others to embrace the wholeness of who they are? Or, do you set about on your life course with a predefined agenda?

Not on the Menu
09/Aug/2017 07:23 AM

There's this one restaurant I go and have breakfast at sometimes. It is kind of a funny place to observe the goings on. The waitresses are all like the proverbial bartenders in that all these guys come in and sit at the counter pouring their hearts out to these ladies. But, the truth be told, you can see that these guys are all dreaming that they were in a relationship with that one particular one. I often wonder if these waitresses even understand what is taking place because they are totally feeding into the narrative, they are so nice and so attentive to these aging men?

For virtually all of my life I've eaten a good portion of my meals in restaurants and I have, occasionally, become friends with some of the staff. In my younger days I even went out with a few of the girls I met in these establishments. At one point in my twenties I was going out with this total Psycho Bitch who got jealous that I was friendly with this one waitress that worked at a restaurant I used to frequent so she got a hold of my credit card and sent her like $500.00 worth of flowers delivered to the café. Embarrassing… There have also been a few very positive things that have happened to me via my interaction with food staff. I met this one girl who was a waitress/actress, gave her a lead role in my Zen Film, _The Hard Edge of Hollywood,_ and she was great! You should check out her performance.

Now, one of things I have long noticed is than many a man does not go into a restaurant simply to get a meal. They have an entirely different set of expectations. When they go into a restaurant and a waitress is nice to them they immediately build up this entire melodrama of possibilities in their mind.

The truth of life is that people are constantly looking to find that mate. This is especially the case if they are not in a relationship or are in a bad relationship. Somehow, the restaurant becomes the logical single's bar for some. But, and this is a big but… What these people are seeking is commonly not going to happen—especially when one is deeper into their life, for then people have history with others, are in relationships, have had children, have been formulated by the positive and more particularly the negative relationship they've had in their past. So, a man may come into an establishment day-after-day, dreaming of finding love with one of the workers, but that's not on the menu. It is not going to happen. Again, I wonder if that is why some of these food servers are so nice and so attentive, they want to make that little bit of extra bank in the form of a tip. I don't know?

In small towns, everybody knows everybody. It large work establishments, where there are a lot of people housed in one facility, everybody knows everybody. But, out in the expanses of the big city, the flavors are constantly changing and the dreams once desired, having often times turned bad, are constantly left behind. Some people are forever on a quest, dreaming that next taste will be the perfect flavor. But, is it? Can it ever be? The illusion of the Out There or the what that person has to offer or the I bet they are the perfect one of me, is only a real as the moment it is fantasied within. Most everybody wants to be with somebody but once they are with them, reality sets in. And, for some, the illusion of the waitress who appears to be nice and listens to the aimless ramblings of a customer is the perfect hotbed for fantasy. But, fantasy is never reality. What you do not know you will never know until you know. And then, what are you left with? Just another relationship with another person who has all of the flaws of everyone else. It is far better to find out what is actually on the menu before you try to get the chef to create something that they do not know how to cook.

Catfishing, Stalking, Disinformation, Fake News, Welcome to the World Wide Web
08/Aug/2017 07:03 AM

Recently, I've been doing several interviews for an upcoming book I've written that's about to be published in Eastern Europe and almost inevitably I am asked questions about what do I think about the internet's role in publishing and its function in information dissemination. From all these questions, it has made me ponder the role of the internet (again).

Certainly, in this day and age, we are all defined by the internet. Me, I was one of the early participants to utilize all it had to offer when it entered the realm of personal computing in the 1980s. In fact, when I wrote my Ph.D. dissertation, I was surprised to find that I did not have to go to libraries for all of my previously published references as I could access some newspaper and academic databases online. But, the internet grew and has continued to grow. As time has gone on I have found that it has become somewhat stagnate in the way it, (and yes, I do see it as an entity onto itself), has come to demarcate its role. Of course, you can still do academic research on the internet, (if you have the mind to), but it is more delineated by personal opinions, unsubstantiated speculations, aberrant misdirected mental pursuits, and fake news than anything else. Yet, here we all are, defined by it.

Mostly, I see it as being used a means for people to not come to terms with the reality of their own life. And, I think this is not a good thing. As I've said a lot of times in a lot of places before, the internet is a realm of fictional reality where no one is truly who they say they are. …People can claim knowledge, can claim title, can present fake personas, can spread lies, can steal, can threaten, can say anything they want to say with little or no consequence as they are nothing in the world of *No Thing Ness.* As there are no repercussions to many of the actions taken on the internet, people feel no necessity to bear any burden of accuracy, verity, truthfulness, or responsible for the results of their internet-based activities. Thus, people live in an altered reality which has no suchness. As we are at a time in history where many people have lived their entire life knowing nothing but life on the internet, they have been guided down a road of false truths, into a sense of non-being. And, not non-being in the spiritual sense but in the anomalous classification.

Now, some may argue this point. And, that's fine, that's your opinion. But, if you are one of those people who tweets, who chats in newsgroups, (that term always amused me because they are anything but), who posts their opinions on the various sites that allow such things, and so on, you are one of the people that has brought the lie into the realms of reality. You are out there in cyberspace stating what you feel and maybe even believing what you say but are you doing any of the actual research that you would have been forced to present in say a required project that you had to turn in for a grade for one of your classes in school? Probably not. You are just rambling your feelings. Which is all fine and good but, again, this goes to the source of my belief that there is currently an elemental problem with the internet. Namely: opinions presented as fact, no true research, and no one being who and what they say they are or taking any responsibility for the karma of their words or actions.

You know, throughout my years on the internet, there have been a lot of people who have cared enough to contact me and we have interacted. Though we may have been continents away from one another, we have developed a positive relationship based upon a common understanding. They ask, I answer. I ask, they answer. Though this is still life defined by the internet, it is interpersonal interaction. From this, (and only from this), truths about thoughts, opinions, philosophies, people, and human understanding can be gained. But, this only occurs via personal communication.

As I have long stated, people who turn to religious figures that they do not and cannot know, truly miss the actual process of spiritual obtainment. If you know your teacher, you can come to understand the flaws of human existence, and from this comprehend that each person, no matter what their spiritual rank, is a human being with the frailties of human existence. This does not mean we cannot learn from that person once we see their flaws; it simply allows us to witness that each person is a unique (and human) entity onto themselves. This is the same with the internet, if you use it as an abstract construct that allows your emotions to run wild, while you live in a reality based upon falsehoods, lies, and altered personalities, than where will your life ultimately end up? What will be the definition of your life?

So, it is to this end, that when I answer the questions that are posed to me as presented in the beginning of this essay, the internet is a great place for the dissemination of studied truths, as presented in books and via other formats, but it is more defined by the mind of the person who does not care enough to reach out to the source of the knowledge or go to the person who possesses a factual basis about the subjects they are discussing. Thus, if we ever hope to focus the internet we each need to care enough to go to the source, ask the questions, get the answers, and then come to a defined genuineness based in a factual reality not solely defined by emotions and unsubstantiated falsities.

* * *
07/Aug/2017 03:34 PM

Why do the people who have done something wrong fight so hard to make themselves look like they are the one in the right?

Nobody Wants to Hear What the Preacher Has to Say Until They Are On Their Deathbed
07/Aug/2017 12:43 PM

If we look around ourselves, everywhere we will find people telling us how we should live. Though the messages vary to a degree, via religious orientation, they basically all say the same thing: be nice, be good, be kind, be forgiving, don't lie, don't hurt people, don't steal, and don't ingest things that are bad for your body. The words are all the same but nobody listens. That is to say, nobody listens until the are up against the wall of death and then they want answers. They want to know why this is happening to them. They want the bad that is happening to them to stop. They turn to the preacher, to the Bible, to the Koran, to the Dhammapada, to their family and friends; they want an answer. But, the answer is obvious, you did what you did and now you are paying the price.

This occurrence does not only happen when someone is dying. The moment a person encounters any intense invasion of negativity into their life they want to know why. But again, it is the same answer, you did what you did and now you are paying the price.

People never look to themselves when they encounter negativity. They never look to what they have chosen to do and what they have chosen to say as the culprit. Instead, they want to blame someone else out there.

The fact is, most people, with any sense of life responsibility, do not intentionally do bad things and/or hurt other people. They simply live their life to the best of their ability. This is one of the main reasons why an individual who is a faith-based person is far less likely to do things that will hurt others. Why? Because they are taught a code of ethics that they understand they must adhere to. But, a large portion of the world is not like this. In fact, most people are solely driven by a sense of self; only desiring what they desire. Thus, their actions give birth to an entire life of negative karma, yet they are too blind to see this and will deny it to their dying day. Then, at their dying day, they turn to the preacher, asking why and begging for his forgiveness. …They are not begging for forgiveness from those they hurt, they are begging forgiveness from the great beyond. But, how does that help anyone they hurt? How does that erase any negative karma?

If we look around ourselves, we can quickly identify the people we know who are self-serving individuals and do not care about the impact they are having on others. Just look at the people you know, which of them takes from another person, which of them says bad things about other people, which of them are judgmental, which of them smokes a cigarette and then throws it on the ground, when they are done, polluting our world? Good is obviously good. Bad is obviously bad.

The work environment is always a good place to study the way other people behave. This is due to the fact that workers are generally put into a space where they interact with people that they would not normally encounter in their day-to-day life. As these people are brought together into one enclosed environment, personalities quickly come into play.

Who have you encountered in your life that you have studied and consciously observed what became of their life due to the way they have interacted with people and with life?

If you watch, you will see. If you watch, you can learn.

From a personal perspective, I have been involved with the film industry for the better part of thirty years. This is one of the most ego-driven, cut throat businesses in the world. I have watched as a few people climbed to the top of the game. Some have done this by walking all over other people—by stealing their ideas, their creations, and making tons-and-tons of money off of the vision of another. I have also watched as some of these people were destroyed; financially and otherwise. Did they learn their lesson and seek forgiveness and invoke recompense? Some did. Some did not. A few, the moment they had the chance, climbed right back on the wagon of thoughtlessness and set about taking from and hurting others once again.

But, this is life. You cannot make another person understand what they are doing is wrong if they do not care. You cannot make another person care about other people if all they think about is themselves. And, this goes to the whole point of this discourse. People are going to live their life the way they are going to live it. They are not going to care until they are forced to care. And then, most likely, they will only care about themselves. So, you can talk to these people; tell them they are doing something wrong. You can preach at these people; tell them they should repent. But, most likely, they are not going to listen. They are not going to listen until they are on their deathbed. Then, instead of caring about anybody else, asking for forgiveness for the sins they committed against other people, they are simply going to think about themselves, wishing their own pain would go away.

So, how are you going to encounter life? If you take from other people, if you make money on the ideas and the creations of others, you owe them everything. Are you going to pay your bill?

If you hurt others, via words or deeds, do you think you will never have a price to pay?

Nobody owes you anything. You do not have the right to hurt or steal from others. Your life and ultimately your death is all based upon what you choose to do each moment of your existence. Where you will end up at the final moments of your life is defined what you did to people; who you hurt, who you helped, and how you behaved in this life place. I can suggest you do good things. I can advise you to help not hurt. I can advocate that you make anything you can better not worse. But, it is you who will have to make the final choice about what you do or do not do, just as it is you who will pay the final price. Think about it…

I Want to Give Somebody a Lucky Day
07/Aug/2017 07:47 AM

I was kicking back having a Macchiato on Saturday afternoon on the patio at one of my local Starbucks. My lady and I were talking about the things that people talk about. As I was sitting there a family of four walks by: two parents, a son and a daughter. The young boy, maybe around nine or ten, takes some change out of his pocket and throws it on the ground, then he continues to walk. The mother hearing this, turns around and tells him to pick it up, probably thinking that the change hitting the ground was an accident. It was not. A stranger walking by begins to pick up the change and hands it to the boy. The young boy exclaims, *"I want to give somebody a lucky day."*

What a nice thought. There he is, this young boy, possessing a vague understanding of life that when you find a penny (or whatever) on the ground that it means good luck. And, he wanted to instigate that good luck in somebody's life.

How much of your time do you spend trying to give somebody a, *"Lucky day?"* Really… How much of your life time do you spend trying to give anybody anything—especially somebody you don't know? Think about it, this really defines who you are as a human being and the effect you are having on the world.

Sadly, most people never think about anybody but themselves and maybe the ones they care about. But, who you care about quite often changes over time. Who cares about you changes over time. But, there is the greater ALL to this equation. If you can give somebody something, somebody that you do not even know—if you can make them feel just a little bit better, if even for a moment, doesn't that make the All better? If you make somebody's life just a slight bit happier, the world becomes a happier/better place.

Try it. The results may amaze you.

* * *
05/Aug/2017 01:36 PM

Everybody has their expectations but think how free your life would become if you had none.

* * *
05/Aug/2017 01:36 PM

The memories of your life only matter to you.

* * *

05/Aug/2017 01:35 PM

Have you ever put your friendships to the test?

Making the Same Mistake Twice
04/Aug/2017 07:04 AM

I forever find it curious how people do the same thing over and over and over again. They do something and they realize it is wrong or someone tells them it is wrong but they do it again. Why can't people learn from their mistakes?

From a psychological perspective, there are a million reasons for this but what they all come down to is two primary elements:

1. a person is simply unconscious of their life, the effect they are having on others or they consciously do not care—they want to hurt themselves and/or other people.

2. a person is trapped into a mindset that may best be described as, "*Stubbornness.*" They believe that they have the right to do anything they want to do and when they don't get their way in doing it they get angry and their rage boils under the surface until they again perform the same action and everyone else be damned.

But, at the root of any, *"Mistake,"* is that the doer either hurts themselves or they hurt someone else. If they hurt themselves, the lesson is generally quickly learned. *"It hurts! I don't want to feel that again."* If they hurt someone else, however, they may not even see it as a mistake. Instead, it may make them gain a sense of empowerment. That is a wrong frame of mind to be operating from of course, yet it is how many people encounter life.

But, let's look at this a little deeper... Why does anyone want to hurt themselves? The simple answer is they get something out of the experience. Whether it is getting high, getting drunk, getting fat, getting laid, getting in a fight, getting a tattoo, spending money they don't have, or smoking, there is an experience that they consider enjoyable associated with the act. It is only at the point when what they have done has equaled something negative in their own life and has caused them to understand that what they did was a, *"Mistake,"* that they take the time to study their actions but then it is too late. The damage has been done.

This same mindset goes to why people invade the life of another person causing damage in their life. They like the experience and perhaps the attention they get from doing what they do. But, isn't it wrong to hurt someone else? No matter what the logic, hurting is hurting. And, if you or someone else does not care about the fact that you are hurting someone what does that say about you and what type of energy do you think that action will bring into your life?

Here lies the ultimate definition of the concept of a, *"Mistake."* A mistake brings a negative reaction to your life and/or to the life of other people.

There is also a certain, *"Victim mentality,"* that exists in the mind of some individuals who perform the action of making mistakes. People do something that is wrong, but when they are called out on it they become the victim. *"Why can't I do what I want to do when I want to do it?"* Now, this goes to all levels of life. From one person who wants to be in a relationship with someone else when the other person does not want the coupling to take place, onto taking, stealing, breaking, making false statements, telling lies, altering the truth, speaking out of turn, and hurting just for the sake of hurting. These can all be called mistakes but, in fact, theses are simply actions that people take without taking the other person (any person) into consideration. In fact, the term, *"Mistake,"* is highly overused. It is simply used when a person does something that hurts themselves or someone else and then that person does not want to take responsibility for their actions.

But, what does this all boil down to as, so-called, mistakes are made all of the time? A mistake is you not existing in a world of caring consciousness. For if you were living in a world defined by focused consciousness you would not be hurting yourself and you would not be hurting others. Thus, there would be no mistakes. This is why the person who renounces the world to embrace true spirituality lets go of as many aspects of the world, desire, and personality as possible. From this, they eliminate many of the life-elements that would cause them to make mistakes in the first place.

For those of us living in the world, what can we do to not make so-called mistakes and to not make the same mistake twice. The answer is care—think about the all, the everything, the everyone. Turn yourself off long enough to see that you matter, that other people matter and that if you hurt them, if you hurt anyone, you hurt yourself because it sets a never-ending pattern of doing to undo the original doing into motion.

Become conscious. Focus. Care. Don't make mistakes. And, never make the same mistake twice.

* * *
03/Aug/2017 11:48 AM

Say something nice and say it loud. See what it will invoke.

*   *   *
03/Aug/2017 11:48 AM

Sometimes the best answer is to shut your mouth, close your eyes, and go to sleep.

* * *

03/Aug/2017 07:57 AM

Can you become more than you were yesterday?

Everybody Thinks They're Right
03/Aug/2017 06:53 AM

When was the last time that you changed your mind about a subject? When was the last time that you believed something about someone or something, actually took the time to researched the subject further, and then came to a new conclusion? How about the people you know, do any of them ever change their mind?

As we pass through life most people come to conclusions based upon very erroneous foundations. They see something, they hear something, they read something, and from this they believe. That's that. Their mind is never changed. Though they may rarely think about the subject, they know what they know. How about you?

Life is a pathway of realization. Some people enter this pathway willingly and are constantly in a state of reevaluating the truth as they believe they know it. The people who encounter life in this manner are few, however. Most people don't even care what the facts are. They just want to believe and once they believe they know they are right and they will fight for what they believe to the end.

The furthermost of the issue takes place when someone believe that they are right, someone questions their genuineness, so that person goes out and finds specious facts to substantiate their storyline. This doesn't make their belief a truth it simply makes it a collaborated falsehood.

Opinion is a condition of humanhood. But, opinion is never fact. You should not allow yourself to become lost in it.

If you are open minded, if you don't bind yourself to what you believe, think about the new experience of realization you can have everyday.

The Contribution You Didn't Make
03/Aug/2017 06:53 AM

Do you ever observe the life of a person who had hoped to achieve a specific something in their life but did not? They are always the ones who are the most critical of those who have achieved the dream they desired. Whether this dream was big or small they wanted to make it theirs. When they did not, all they are left with is demeaning criticism.

As is obviously the case, critiquing what someone else has done is far easier than doing something yourself. Criticizing someone for the way they have done what they have done takes very little effort. Even those who make a living out of reviewing the creations of others also fall prey to the reality of the fact that they are not the actual doer and, as such, they are simply the talker about those people who have done what they have achieved. Thus, they have branded themselves simply someone who talks about others as they are not focused enough to make the dream their own.

When we are young we each hope to achieve a certain something in our lives. Generally, when we are young, these dreams are grandiose. From this, comes idol worship—loving the rock star, the movie star, the sports star, or the guru. Some of us, as we pass through life, work very hard to achieve the dream of becoming something like the person we admire. This is how those who rise to the pinnacle of their craft get there—they see it, they envision it, and then they work at making it happen. But, the fact is, nobody achieves all of their dreams. Even for those who appear to have actualized their dream, the dream lived is never that which was imagined. None-the-less, through effort and hard work, making one's dream a reality did occur in the lives of some people.

For those who have not achieved the life of success they had hoped, do they ever look at themselves as being the cause? Do they ever question why they did not make their dream a reality? I suppose in each case this is different. But, what most never realize or never want to admit to themselves is that it was they, themselves, and their lack of focused concentration that kept from achieving, at least at a small level, what they aspired to. From this, some are driven to the world of being dominated by a critical mind.

From a psychological and metaphysical perspective, it is commonly understood that what you focus upon, you bring into your life. You manifest what is in your mind. If all you do is focus on what others have achieved and how you do or do not like it, then all you have done is cast your own mind to a never-ending cycle of debate that never equals you actually achieving what you hope to achieve. From this, at best, all you do is cause more attention to be brought to the life and the achievements of the person you are criticizing.

So, what is the answer? The answer is simple, ask yourself, *"What do you want to achieve?"* Be realistic about this question. Now, ask yourself, *"What can I do to make it happen?"* Once you have defined this, stop getting in your own way by focusing on the life of someone else—especially via negativity. Get out there, draw up a precise game plan, and everyday work towards making your dream a reality.

*   *   *

02/Aug/2017 06:44 AM

Why do so many people embrace negativity? Because they are dissatisfied with their life.

* * *
02/Aug/2017 06:43 AM

Why does no one blame god?

*   *   *
02/Aug/2017 06:41 AM

How much of what you do is based upon what was done to you?

*   *   *
02/Aug/2017 06:40 AM

Just because your next-door neighbor is quiet that does not mean that you are not loud.

*   *   *

02/Aug/2017 06:40 AM

Can you become more than the people you worship?

* * *
02/Aug/2017 06:39 AM

Do you ever blame other people for the sins you've committed?

The Melodrama and the Nothing
01/Aug/2017 07:50 AM

Has anyone ever done something bad to you and then when they were presented with this fact that attempted to play the victim? They instigated it, they did it, yet now, somehow, you are the one at fault.

Have you ever tried to help someone—you really went out of your way to do something nice for them and then they turned the whole situation around and somehow, at least in their mind, you came out the bad guy? They told the world you did something wrong.

Life is dominated by interpersonal perceptions. Life is dominated by how people want to be perceived by others. Life is dominated by how one person feels about another person—whether what they are feeling is based upon fact or fiction.

How do you encounter life? Is it a peaceful process of transitioning from one life experience to the next? Or, do you create melodrama at each juncture?

How you perceive yourself preceding through reality is what you project to the world. Many people are so lost in their definition of self that they cannot take others into consideration as they encounter life, live their life, and interact with other people. If you are locked into a world based only upon you then your world is a very selfish place. From this, all it becomes is a world defined by how you feel about a specific person or a specific situation and how you want others to perceive you in association with that other specific person or situation.

People who operate from this mindset have a desired outcome for each situation and interpersonal interaction they encounter as they pass through life. They want it to be the way they want it to be. When things are altered, to whatever degree, they then lash out. But, what they rarely or ever do is to take the other person into consideration. They only think about themselves, what they wanted, what they are receiving, and how they can alter the narrative to their own point of view.

Do most people really care what another person is experiencing in life? If you personally know them, maybe you do. If you care about them, maybe you do. If you think or fantasize you can get something from them, maybe you do. But, what about the person next door who is dying from cancer? What about the person across town who has just been attacked by an assailant? What about the person that you do not like what they did to you—no matter what the reason is they did it? Do you care?

How do you feel when someone shifts the storyline and creates melodrama in your life? How do you feel when someone hurts you? How do you feel when someone did not take you into consideration when they did what they did? Now, how do other people feel when you do this to them?

If you want to be whole in life, you must care about other people. You must be willing to turn down your own desires long enough to take the other person, who they are and why they are doing what they are doing, into consideration. Why must you do this? Because it makes everything in everyone's life better.

Make things better not worse.

* * *
01/Aug/2017 07:29 AM

Say something positive when someone else is saying something negative.

*   *   *
01/Aug/2017 07:29 AM

If you don't know what you're looking for you can never find it.

* * *
30/Jul/2017 05:54 PM

When you reach judgement day how will you be judged, by those you helped or by those you hurt?

All It Costs is Money
30/Jul/2017 08:46 AM

In life, a good percentage of what we all want is based upon money. Maybe you want a specific car, home, camera, guitar, bicycle, suit, dress, purse, pair of shoes, vacation, you name it—all based upon if you do or do not have the money to buy it.

Some people base their life upon credit cards. Don't do it! Not only do you pay insane rates of interest—meaning everything you buy costs you way more than its actual price but having unsecured debt is life debilitating—it holds your everything back from becoming.

Same with student loans… Every person I have ever known who has taken one out was all happy about it, believing they found a way to get over on the system and climb to the top of the heap via a college degree but all they did was bind themselves to a seemingly endless/never ending payment at the end of every month.

But then, there are those people with money. Again, it takes money to get what you want to make things happen. You can't be a filmmaker without a camera, can you? I have watched as many people I have known, by whatever method, purchased their camera, computer, and filmmaking equipment, all with the dreams of making a movie but then nothing… They did not make a film. …Even though they had the money to buy the necessary items, they did not possess the focus and the drive to actually get out there and make it happen.

I think back to a funny story… When I was teaching a course at U.C.L.A. this one young lady student of mine bought the top of the line DV camera of the time. We got to be friends and as I was putting together a new film I asked her if she wanted to be the DP (Director of Photography). I thought it would be fun to have my movie filmed from a new and different perspective; that of a woman. She accepted my offer. On the night before the shoot was to begin she contacted me and wanted to have a sit down. Sure, that was normal. I thought we are going to discuss some of the shooting style. When I arrived we sat down and began our conversation. She said, *"I have one question, how do you focus the camera?"* What! Obviously, I had to push back the production and find another DP. It's funny now. But, it's things like that can really mess up the scheduling of the cast and the crew and make the filmmaker lose credibility.

But, here we are… She had the money but not the determination to learn the craft. For example, me, when I get a new camera I immediately drop everything and learn all about it. But, not all people operate from that perspective.

And, this goes to the point of all this… Have you ever really wanted something, found a way to buy it, and then never used it or it did not equal the pathway to your fulfillment as you had intended? I believe that most of us have had that experience to varying degrees. So, what does this tell us about desire and the price of that desire?

Desire costs money. More than just money, desire costs you Life Time. Meaning, you must find a way to buy your desire, pay for the ongoing costs of your desire, and then pay for the consequences of your desire.

Most of us what to do something in life. Many of us what to create something in life. Almost universally these things cost money. You should really calculate the long-term cost(s) of your desires before you set about on the course of purchasing that desire. Desires are never free.

The Evolution of Innocence
29/Jul/2017 07:10 AM

As we pass through life we are continually adding to our resume. From the moment we are born we experience new things every day. The more we experience, the more we want to experience. From this, the mind of many becomes addicted to experiencing. Also, from this, people develop the emotion of boredom when they are not experiencing. They want to see, feel, and experience something new.

Our life is set forward by what we experience. From what we experience we develop the illusion of opinions. But, opinions are not fact—they are not even a stationary form of understanding because with each new experience opinions evolve and change. Yet, people come to base their life experiences upon their opinions as those opinions cause them to pursue curtain avenues in their life.

Think back to when you were young. Remember the amazement of all that was new. Watching the clouds in the sky. Studying the waves as they hit the shore. Experiencing the rain falling onto your head. Jumping into a swimming pool. Flying a kite. Today, do you find wonderment by looking at the clouds in the sky? Is it an amazing feeling to jump in a pool? Do you ever even think about flying a kite?

From time and experience comes the loss of the innocence of experiencing. Things become known and expected. Some experiences become loved and sought after while other experiences are forcefully forgotten and avoided at all costs. Though this is the common course of the experiential life of most people; the innocence of the pure, the good, and the wonderful does not have to be lost. It can be consciously reembraced.

Step beyond your thinking mind. Step beyond what you know you know. Forget all you believe that you like and dislike and take a walk back into your innocence. Experience things new and for the first time. Look up to the sky and embrace the wonderment of watching the cloud move through the sky as their forms constantly change.

*   *   *

28/Jul/2017 06:03 PM

Instead of simply believing everything you see, read, or hear, why don't you actually look for the truth?

Losing Someone
28/Jul/2017 05:24 PM

Have you ever lost someone you truly cared about? Meaning, has anyone you truly loved died?

If you have lost someone you truly care about, then the rest of your life has been changed forever. If you have not, you remain in a state of sterilized emotions.

As we pass through life there are some people that we truly love. They become a part of who we truly are.

Many of us find love in the form of people. This is the accepted standard for love. Someone comes into our life and, for whatever reason, we come to love them. With them, we are better people. Without them, we are less.

Some of us additionally find love in the form of pets. For anyone who has never had a pet, they truly do not understand how they are a personality driven human being hiding in a furry form. Thus, they cannot understand. But, for anyone who has partnered with a pet, you understand how they become an essential part of your life. They love you unconditionally.

Sadly, the life of most furry friends is not as long as that of a human. Thus, they will most likely pass away before you. If you truly loved them, this can be devastation; leaving any person far less than when that friend was alive.

If you have not experienced this loss of loved-life, human or otherwise, then you do not understand existence. This is why so many people walk though their younger years very cavalier. They have not lost anyone they truly loved. But, as is the case with most of our lives, we will encounter a time when we lose someone we truly care about. Then, our life will be forever altered. We will see things from a totally different point of view. From this, whenever we think of that life or are reminded of that life, a sadness over takes us.

Some people never have family that they truly love. This is sad. Some people never find relationships where they truly love the other person. Again, sad. Some people never find the love of a pet. Sad… For once you have truly loved, your entire being is changed. You no longer only think about yourself but you are allowed to embrace the understanding that there is a greater substance to human existence and that substance is the love of another.

If you understand what I am speaking of, then you understand. And, if you have lost someone, you know the never-ending pain of that loss. If you do not, some would say you are lucky. But, I would say that you have not touched the essence of life as you have not understood the depths of death.

Life is a finite timespan defined only by what we feel and what we do while we are alive in the body that we have. Look around you. Do you love? Do you love totally? Now, look outside yourself. Look to the people you know—study how they behave. Do they love? Do they love totally?

Love is the basis for the true understanding of life. If you love, if you have loved, then you know what I mean. If you have lost someone you love than you have a profound understanding of existence and this knowledge causes you to behave in a defined manner.

Seek love. Know love. Seek out those who understand and embrace love. And, your everything becomes better.

* * *

28/Jul/2017 03:01 PM

You never know a person's true nature until they have failed at what they hoped to achieve.

Freaks, Freak Out
28/Jul/2017 01:17 PM

There is something very magical about the inner-city. Especially the inner-city on the wrong side of the tracks. Yeah, yeah, it's dangerous. You never know who your friends are or aren't. But, there is magic.

Today, I was over there doing as I do. And, I hear the song, "*Le Freak,*" by Chic in the not too far off distance. The sound of the song kept getting closer.

Soon, I see this guy riding one of those three-wheeled bicycles. In the basket in the center of the two rear wheels he had a gigantic boom box. Now, keep in mind, this is not the late 1970s or the early 1980s. This is 2017. But, there he was peddling along with his boom box blasting.

The man had a large black afro and a totally grey goatee. Quite a sight.

That's a great song, as he got closer I could not help but dance a little bit.

As he rode by, I gave him a nod and we smiled at each other. Inspiring…

You know, it is those abstract moments in life that truly give you a reason to be inspired.

When I got back into my car I had to call up that song and dance in my seat as I drove along.

It is Easy to Criticize When You Haven't Lived the Life
28/Jul/2017 08:50 AM

Having been involved in the film industry for almost three decades at this point in my life I can say with certainty that most people who are not here in Hollywood (and I use Hollywood as a generic term) have no idea what is actually taking place. They have not tried to get an agent, they have not paid a lot of money to get their headshots photographed and run, they have not been to a casting session, they have not paid a lot of money to take acting classes, they have not had people lie to them; promising them the world. They have not even cared enough to move to Hollywood and actually give the industry a try. Yet, they have all of these ideas and opinions about what is taking place. But, they have no idea! They have no basis for their thoughts. What is taking place in the Midwest in a film class at a college campus is not what goes on out here.

Some people want to believe that their opinions matter. And, maybe to them and their friends it does. But, as in all areas of life, if you have not lived it, you do not know what you are taking about.

Having grown up in Hollywood (literally) I saw a lot of what the industry did to people. That's why I steered my life away from it initially. But, when I did get involved, I jumped in head first. And, just like all the others, who come from all across the globe, I too fell prey to a lot of the illusion Hollywood has to offer. But, that's why I can comment on the subject. I have been here. I have lived it. Have you?

When I evolved into being a filmmaker this is also why I developed Zen Filmmaking. As I state over-and-over again, I did it to simplify the filmmaking process so people could actual get their films made. Again, as I state over-and-over again, this is also why I generally cast unknown actors and actresses in my films, I want to give them the chance to actually be in a film—a chance that no one else will offer them. To all the critics, what are you offering them but words?

Hollywood is all about the promises. It is about the, *"I will do this for you."* But, this very rarely ever happens. What Hollywood is really all about is the lie. Most people come out here believing the dream and eventually leave to go back home very disappointed. I say this, as someone who actually knows. And, I say this to make people understand the reality.

Now, you can criticize me all you want. You can love or hate my Zen Films, I don't care. But, if you have not been here, if you have not lived the life, you <u>do not,</u> you <u>cannot</u> understand what I base my words upon. So, before you start throwing shots, live the life. Then, you will have a basis for what you say. If not, you are just like every other armchair quarterback who believes they have all of the answers to the game but has never even been on the field.

Anger as a Tool
28/Jul/2017 08:12 AM

Many people believe that by becoming angry and expressing that anger in a boisterous manner that action will cause them to get what they want. Generally, they do this to another person as a show of power, force, and might. They may yell, they may scream, they may break things all to make a situation turn out the way they want it to turn out. But, is this the action of a conscious person?

Most people who express their anger in a less than ideal manner are dominated by their anger. Somebody has done something that they don't like which causes them to go into a rage. From this, all kinds of inappropriate actions are unleashed. But, what is the motivating factor for any of this? The answer is that one person wants something to be done in a different manner than it is being performed and they are willing to go to any lengths to make that thing happen the way they want it to happen.

Anger is expressed in all realms of life. Certainly, interpersonal relationships are at the forefront of the expression of anger. This is due to the fact that when two (or more) people possess a very close interactive association they become hyper aware of how the other person is behaving and whether or not they approve of that behavior. Thus, this is where a lot of relationship fights are born.

The workplace is also a hotbed for the expression of anger. One person who believes they are in control wants one of their subordinates to do something in the way they want it to be done. When it is not, this may cause an explosion of anger.

But, what does an explosion of anger actually equal? Generally, all it does is to damage the life of both the angered person and especially the life of the person who this anger is focused upon. Yes, perhaps the person who goes into a rage may get the other person to do things the way they want those things to be done but in the process, that have hurt the life of that other individual and caused a lot of resentment.

When anger is enacted it proves that the person who is raging cares more about themselves than the person they are mad at. They care more about what they are feeling and what they want than what is going on with the other person. In fact, when someone is mad at someone else they generally are not even considering that other person's point of view. All they want is what they want and they are willing to explode to get it.

A person who embraces explosive anger possess a mind that they are not in control of. They allow their emotions to control them instead of being the master of themselves. The sourcepoint for most people who embrace explosive anger can be traced back to their childhood where they learned that if the scream long and hard enough they will get what they want. But, whatever the cause, outwardly expressed anger delineates a person who is not in control of themselves and does not care about the other person.

In life, each of us experiences anger. Certainly, people do bad things to other people. They hurt them, they steal from them, they don't consider how their actions are affecting them, they invade their life, they break their heart, and the list goes on. All of these things may cause the average person to become angry. But, it is what we do with that anger that defines us as a human being.

For some of us, due to our psychological programing in the early stages of our life, we must learn how to gain control over our anger and not let it become a dominating, expressive force in our life. But, even if this is the case, it is the person themselves who is the source of their anger and how they express it.

Each person decides what to like and what to hate. Each person decides what makes them happy and what makes them sad. Each person decides what gives them a sense of elation and what makes them angry. Think about this, is you didn't care about a particular subject or the way a particular person was behaving, would you have any reason to become anger? Probably not. Thus, if you can be whole enough in yourself to not care about what another person is doing or how they are behaving you will never have a reason to become angry. From this, you will not hurt the life of the person you are angry at and you will not hurt your own evolution by unleashing negative deeds based upon your anger.

When the Art Has Been Discarded
28/Jul/2017 07:01 AM

It always surprises me when I find works of art that have been discarded. Whether this is in a thrift store or a garbage pile, I always wonder why it was created, why it was loved or hated, and then why no one cared about it anymore to the degree that it was simply thrown away.

Over the past weekend I was a that this one shop that sells unique pieces of everything that people can use to create works of art. As I was walking into the shop I noticed that there was a large pile of paintings created on paper. They were mostly faces and bodies painted in what could best be described as the abstract impressionistic style. They were really good. I really liked them.

Then, I began to question, why would anybody discard all of these paintings? They were obviously all done by the same artist. I looked but there was no signature so I could not track the artist down. Did the person die? Had they given them to a lover and the relationship went bad so the person gave them all away? Did the artist, them self, no longer want them? Maybe they had some deep realization about something and they had moved along? I will never know. But, there they all sat in an unloved pile.

I thought to buy one or two of my favorites but as they were all together in a stack of maybe one-hundred I realized that would not be right as they were all so perfectly linked in a discord of harmony. Then I thought to buy them all. But, I realized I have collected so much art over the years that I do not have the space to display most of it and that would not be right to just hide it away. So, I took a few photographs and I left all of those works of art for a better person than me. I hope they all find a home because they were very-very good. And, for the artist, I hope all is well with their life and they are still painting as they have a great talent that should not simply be lost to the discarded pile of art in life.

Every Creator Says the Same Thing
27/Jul/2017 09:17 AM

It always strikes me that whenever I see or hear a musician, a filmmaker, or an author being interviewed they each discuss the same issue. That issue is how they are frustrated with the way people believe they have the right to take their creations, utilize them as they see fit, and even, in some cases, redistribute them and make money off of that item without ever paying for that service. They each believe the same thing, (as do I), that if the people who are taking the creations of others, for free, actually were they ones who created them they would have a very different perspective as to what was taking place.

This phenomenon of, *"Digital Stealing,"* began very recently when one looks to the overall view of human history. I mean, just a couple of decades ago it was far too expensive to do any of that. People could not make a copy of a film, even duping large scale copies of video tapes was far to expensive. To rerecord and then repress a music album cost far too much money to make it a viable commodity. Books… Forget about it. To actually copy, type set, and then print a book was very expensive so it wasn't done. But, in the digital age this has all changed.

When I taught classes on filmmaking in the late 1990s and even into the early 2000s I used to warn my students about placing their screen credits in white on black cards at the beginning and at the end of their production. As what used to happen, particularly in the Asian market place, was that unscrupulous distributors would take the film, remove the screen credits and add their own. It happened to me. This is why I told them, if they could afford it, to put the credits over picture as this was a way of assuring that even if the movie was stolen the true credits would remain intact.

But now, here you and I sit at our computers. The world is our oyster. And many, if not most, people do not even care about what they are doing to the creative works of others as long as they can do it for free. Some have even found a way of making money off of the creations of others. Do you ever think about this as you walk through your pathway of life and you take advantage of what others have created? Do you ever stand up for the rights of the creator?

I believe that each of us who walks the path of creativity wants to get our creations out to the masses. If we didn't, we would be creating them in the first place. Nobody writes a book with the hopes that no one will read it. But, throughout history there has always been an exchange for goods and services rendered. This hasn't always been via money. But, this system has always been in place. It has always been in place until now—in this current time frame we are living within.

It has always been the youth of society that has pushed the levels and understanding of human consciousness forward. This is because when you are young you have the time and the freedom to explore new realms of possibilities as you are not yet burdened by many of the responsibilities of latter life. But, this is also the time period when many people make the biggest mistakes in their life. They set themselves into a course of action that will come to define the rest of their life. Good or bad, this is just the way it is. But, also good or bad, in youth few people have the ability to look at the big picture and see or care how what they are doing is setting the stage for not only their own life but the lives of others.

If all of the people who are actually the, *"Creators,"* of things have the same problem with what is taking place, doesn't that tell you something? Doesn't that make you think?

The fact is, not everyone takes what is out there in cyber space for free. Some people are very honest. How about you? Do you take for free and feel that you have the right to do it? Do you take for free and feel that just because this other person you know is doing it, that it's okay? Or, do you actually make money off of the creations of other people? If you do, don't you feel you own that person something? Wouldn't it be the right thing to do to pay them, in some shape or form, for what you have taken?

I always go back to the point that all of life begins with you. What you do has the potential to affect the entire world. The small things you do can progress and equal the big things. So, what do you do? Do you take for free and not even care about the consequences? Think about this, if you care enough about the person who created that thing you are stealing to make them the focus of your actions, don't you think that you should care enough about that person to not steal from them in the first place?

Think about what you do. Care about the creators.

Changing the Focus
27/Jul/2017 07:23 AM

    Have you ever noticed how some people are always taking about someone else? Why do they do this? Whether they are doing this knowingly or not, they do this to take the focus off of themselves. As they continually change the focus of the conversation to make the minds of the people they are speaking with focus on the life, words, and actions of someone else, the focus is never turned to them. From this, they are allowed to pass through life without encountering negative criticism. Attack others before they have the chance to attack you.

    Have you ever noticed how some people believe that what they are doing is good or holy but what other people are doing is wrong and sinful? *"I don't drink. That is bad. The world is full of drunks. I don't smoke. That is bad. People are killing the body that god gave them. I don't watch adult movies. That is bad. Lust is not how god would want us to behave. I don't listen to that style of music. It is bad. Rock n' Roll is the devil's music."* And, the list of what they disapprove of goes on—from the large to the small. But, when you confront them about something that they are doing that may be hurting their own body or be damaging the life of someone else they always have an excuse ready to justify their actions. Again, by taking the focus off of themselves and placing the blame elsewhere many people listen to and believe their words.

    In professional magic, (not elemental magic), one of the key factors is that you take the focus of the viewer off of what they are seeing. From this, the magician is allowed to invoke an illusion and perform a magic feat. This is what some people do throughout their life. They make you look over there, instead of looking directly at them. From this, they become the person who guides the conversation. This is also the technique by which many a cult or world leader has risen to prominence.

All of these actions are based in the concept of making other people believe what one person believes. This one person gains followers yet most of these leaders will claim that they are not attempting to do that at all. In fact, some of these people may not even be self-aware enough to realize what is going on. But, most people are not mentally wily enough to see what is happening to them as they begin this path to discipleship. They have fallen into the troop, they have become a disciple, and they did not even realize this was happening to them. Though, just like the teacher, they will most likely claim this is not the case. But, denial is only denial, it is never based in truth.

Why does this process take place in life? Why do people become unknowing disciples of people? They do this because they seek acceptance from someone, out there. They want to become a part of something, out there. And, they do this without even a conscious understanding of their actions. By allowing someone who is bold enough to step to the forefront and guide the conversation all anyone has done is to accept and participate in the direction of a conversation that was instigated by another person. From this, they become part of the greater whole of whatever group they are involved in and they do not have to think for themselves.

Do you think for yourself? Or, do you follow the words instigated by another?

* * *
27/Jul/2017 07:23 AM

Just because you are saying what you are saying with a smile on your face does not mean that what you are saying is nice.

What You Are Looking For
26/Jul/2017 04:36 PM

Each of us comes at life defined by what we expect. Expectations are what drives us to quest for what we desire. From a humanistic and/or spiritual perspective, one will say that you should never enter into any situation with a predetermined judgment but instead allow all things to be as they are—new and fresh. From this, each of these things are allowed to be perfect in their own essence. I would say this too. But, the fact is, most people do not have a highly develop mind. In fact, they don't want to develop their mind. They don't want to, because their mind is already made up.

With a made up mind everything a person enters into is defined by what has taken place in the before. Everything they see, everything they witness, and everything they choose to do is defined by the experiences they previously possessed going into any of these activities. Not good, but this is the way most people encounter their life. Do you?

The problem that exists, when you live your life from this perspective, is that nothing is new or fresh. It is not free. And, as such, you will never enter into one of those peak experience moments where *Satori* is allowed to overtake you. Thus, your life becomes stagnate and the same.

Think about the last time you went to a movie. What were your expectations? Were you expecting it to be as good as that great movie you saw last week or last year? Or, were you going into it knowing that it could never be as great as that movie. In either situation, you entered the movie theater defined by what you had previously viewed. Thus, unless something truly shook you to your core, you were doing nothing more than comparing that experience to a previously lived experience. Thus, you brought all of your mental baggage along with you. From this, any perfection of the moment was lost. How often do you do this?

I used the example of a movie, but this same predefined judgmental mindset can go to all areas of your life. From surfing, to bowling, to going to the supermarket, to going out to dinner, to reading a book.

…Speaking of reading a book, I can tell you a couple of funny stories…

Recently, in this blog, I discussed how a person made a very opinionated documentary about me about five years ago and recently re-released it causing me to receive undeserved hate mail and stuff like that. In that documentary, the documentarian quoted from two of my books on filmmaking. I guess the person got pissed off at me and took those books and some of my films and sold them to a local used bookshop. A university student who was into what I do noticed the transaction, altered me to it, and I own the aforementioned books. I just relooked at them and it was very enlightening to me in that I could see what passages this person had highlighted in yellow. As I stated in a previous blog, those books were designed to help the independent filmmaker but what this person had done was to remove passages from the greater text, which not only made me look bad but completely distorted Zen Filmmaking and what I was hoping to present in those writings. Looking at this person's highlights I could totally see what they were doing. They were not reading the book(s) as a method to learn new knowledge or to be helped in the practice of filmmaking but as a means to find a method to use my own words to make their preconceived notions about me a reality and to make me look bad. Not cool! But, it was/is truly interesting to witness how this person's mind works.

The fact is, this is how many people's minds work. They go into a subject with a preconceived notion about what is presented and they never step out of their own opinions to the degree where they can find a new and perhaps better way of thinking.

Another revealing story, in regard to me, is that when I was in my later thirties I had decided to go back to grad school and earn another Master's Degree. I was taking a course on Comparative Religion as Presented in Literature and one of my assignments was to write a paper about this one teacher/author. Going into the assignment I had never really like the method of this man's presentations as he took a little bit of this religion here and a bit of that philosophy there and then intermingled them in his writings. I read the assigned books and, complete with footnotes, I detailed my appraisal of this man's writings. My instructor rejected the paper, however, and told me to rewrite it as what I had written was far too opinionated and at the graduate level this style of writing was unacceptable. Thus, I had to reset my mind and prepare another twenty-page paper. What happened during this process, however, was I turned off my previously decided upon opinions. When I did, I found that the man had a lot of interesting principals to present. Thus, through my being force to rethink my original beliefs about the man and his writing style I was allowed to come to a new and deeper understanding about life, philosophy, and the way in which we each interpret our lives and the lives of others. It was very enlightening and I am so thankful my instructor forced me to rewrite that paper. If I can find it, perhaps I will present it here somewhere on scottshaw.com.

The point being, if you go into any subject—anything in life with a preconceived notion then you rob yourself of all that situation has to teach you and the sheer beauty and the newness of that experience is lost. This is what I teach in Zen Filmmaking and this is what I suggest in all levels of life. Allow yourself to be free. Allow your mind to not already be made up. From this, a whole world of NEW is allowed to be given birth to. Check it out. You may like it. ☺

* * *
26/Jul/2017 02:31 PM

It is almost impossible to make someone understand the truth when they don't care about the truth.

*   *   *
26/Jul/2017 02:30 PM

When you've created nothing, no one can criticize you.

* * *

26/Jul/2017 07:55 AM

Do you want to know the definition of your life?

Question: *Do you think about you first or do you think about the other person first?*

* * *
26/Jul/2017 07:55 AM

Do you wake up when the dream is over?

Tell Me Who You Are. Tell Me What You're About.
26/Jul/2017 07:53 AM

Who I am/what I am is very obvious. Read the books I have written, read my bio, my blog, and you will know a lot about me and the way I think. But, who are you?

We are overrun with a world of people basing their entire life upon a screen name. In some cases, people use an actual name as their screen name but who knows if that name is even real?

People spout all of these self-conceived notions and judgments on the world of the internet but are they even anywhere close to real? If you don't know who the person actually is who is writing them, what their background is, why the are saying what they are saying, you don't know anything about them so do they have any possibility of being real and true? Stop lying and stop hiding!

In the world of real there is real. You sit down and you tell a person who you are, how you feel, and why you think the way you think. That is reality. That is truth. You did not hide behind the guise of the world wide web. You sat down and actually communicated.

In life, there is only one real and that real is reality. It is face-to-face. It is not hidden by excuses or promises that you say you are who you are when there is no way of proving it.

If you are not real, you are not known, then your life and all you say is nothing more than illusion. From illusion all you say has no meaning or validity for it is all based in a lie.

Do you like to be lied to? If not, enter the world of reality and tell the world who you truly are.

Your Made Me Mentally Ill
25/Jul/2017 07:15 AM

The majority of the world's populous is born into this world with an accepted level of intelligence and they possess the skillset to move through their life in an acceptable manner. Though a small subset or people are born with various levels of mental illness such as schizophrenia and others are born with differing levels of autism these people are in the minority. As such, there exists an established level of what may be considered normal behavior.

Though the exact definition of normal behavior has been debated since the dawn of human consciousness and certain people, in all eras, have pushed the boundaries of accepted normality causing it to evolve. None-the-less, humanity is still defined by a clear sense of what is right and what is wrong and the parameters for how one should behave are clearly delineated.

All this being said, look at how many people are suffering in the world from psychological illnesses. These disorders come in all shapes and sizes from anxiety, to panic attacks, paranoia, phobias, onto personal choices in human behavior like rudeness, grumpiness, promiscuity, and interpersonal violence. But, what is the commonality of all of these psychological conditions? That commonality is that the people who are afflicted with these conditions were not born with them. They were introduced to them at the hands of their family, their friends, their teachers, their religious leaders, their lovers, or society. Thus, someone out there hurt them to the degree that they were shifted from living a normal mental existence. Thus, their mental illness was created by someone out there.

Each person is a unique vessel. Each person processes a personal reality with their own unique criteria for understanding. This is why some people handle things like stress far better than others. What will destroy one person will simply make the next person grow angry. This is humanity. This is life. This is human consciousness.

Again, this brings us back to the point, that no matter how a person personally reacts to a traumatic even that takes place in their life, that initial event was not introduced by themselves. That event was brought on by someone else, someone out there.

Certainly, once an individual has been indoctrinated into a specific aberrant frame of mind they may then act out on that mindset. It has been well documented that once an individual has been damaged by a specific negative event in their life that they may then go out and invoke a similar event onto the life of others. But, the sourcepoint for this is the same. Somebody did something to someone that made them move into a state of mental crisis where they are no longer behaving in an acceptable manner.

Look around you. How many people do you know that behave in an unacceptable manner? How many people do you know that are psychologically damaged and are forced to go to a mental health professional and/or take medication to make them feel okay? How about you? How well have you been adapted into life? Do you have any lingering psychological issues? If you do, then you will understand that they were brought to you by the actions of others. From this, how do you treat others? Do you do things that will cause disharmony and perhaps mental illness in the life of another person? If you do, shame on you!

All of the life we live is a projection of what we have experienced. If we have experienced a good and caring, nurturing existence we are far more likely to be a well-balanced individual. If, on the other hand, we have encountered a lot of trauma, brought to us by the hands of others, then we may have well been introduced to a life defined by psychological abnormality.

At the heart of all life is how you react to what has been done to you. If you have been hurt or damaged by the actions of others, as many of us have, first you need to recognize what is going on with your life and why you are feeling what you are feeling and doing what you are doing. You will then most likely need to get some help to bring your betterment into a clear focus. But then, it all comes down to you. How do you treat others? Do you do things that will create mental trauma in the life of other people? If you do; stop it! If someone says that what you are doing is hurting them or damaging their life be human enough to stop doing it! Understand that the primary cause of why people suffer psychologically is due to the fact of what others have done to them and from this use it as tool to make sure that you never hurt anyone.

*   *   *

24/Jul/2017 01:58 PM

Sometimes you have to do something that is wrong to learn what is right.

* * *
24/Jul/2017 06:54 AM

All bad things that take place in the world begins with one person thinking one bad thought and then expressing that thought to someone else.

* * *
23/Jul/2017 08:28 PM

Your life is defined by whom you have hurt.

Self Sacrifice
23/Jul/2017 08:20 PM

How much do you focus your life upon Self Sacrifice? Meaning, how much of your Life Time do you spend helping and giving to others?

Very few people spend any amount of their Life Time giving to others. There are some who donate their old clothing or furniture to clarities—some occasionally help out a friend move or paint their house but none of this is Self Sacrifice, none of this is Selfless Service. This is simply taking care of you while you help out someone you care about. Giving to charities equals a tax deduction. Helping a friend is doing something that keeps your relationship solid as they will later help you. But, Self Sacrifice involves an entirely different set of parameters. It involves giving to others and helping others when there is nothing in it for you.

The first thing many, if not most, people will ask is, *"Why should I help anybody to the degree that I am doing something that I do not really want to do—why should I help them when I receive no benefit from the giving?"* This is selfishness! There is no other way to spell it out. But, this is how the majority of the world operates. They only do when the doing benefits themselves.

The problem with living your life from this level of consciousness is that no one is ever truly helped. The people that need help are not extended that helping hand and you gain nothing, physically, emotionally, or karmically as all you have done is think about yourself.

Think to your life; how many times have you actually done something for someone when there was no benefit it that deed for you? How many times have you cared more about someone else other than yourself—someone that you did have an interpersonal relationship with? How many times have you cared enough to care enough to turn off your desires, your emotions, what you feel you want and/or deserve and actually do for another person? Have you ever done anything like that?

I believe in most people lives they will conclude that they have never put themselves on hold and given all that it took to make another person's life actually better. Thus, they have never truly helped anybody. And, this is just sad! This is why so many people are suffering in the world. This is why so many people are hurt.

Now, think about this… How many times have you done something that hurt someone else? And, you did it knowing the ultimate consequences, yet you did not care because that doing made you feel better or made your life better? I believe you will be able to remember several times when you have acted in this manner—helped yourself while it hurt someone else.

I realize these words are for the most part falling to deaf ears. Because nobody cares enough to care about the other person. Instead, they find reasons to justify their selfish actions.

I can also point to the times when you have been hurt, when somebody did not care about how you were feeling or did not come to your aid when you needed help. But, instead of using this as a motivating factor to do good, most people simply see this as a reason to travel along the path that they are on only doing for themselves and/or those they care about.

Have you ever wondered why so many people suffer for a long time before they die and ultimately die a very painful death? Karma. As they did not pay for their bad or selfish deeds in life, that toll is taken upon them as they pass towards death.

Life is your choice. Everything that you do is done because you have made a choice to do the something that you set up in that moment where you currently find yourself. What you did yesterday sets your today in motion.

What did you do yesterday? Did you help anybody? Did you care about anybody?

Now, here is an important thing to keep in mind as you pounder these thoughts… Many people think and say that they have scarified for their family or their children. That doesn't count. That is expected—especially in the case of children. You chose to have a child. As you did choose to have that child you then took on the responsibility of giving that child the best life possible. This is also the same with husbands, wives, boyfriends, girlfriends, and lovers. You chose them, they chose you. Thus, whatever you do for them is expected.

What Self Sacrifice and Selfless Service is all about is doing for that person out there who needs your help. It is about turning yourself off and caring more about that other person than you getting what you want. It is about helping. It is about giving.

You can go through your life any way you want. Your life is your choice. But, though what you are doing for yourself may feel good today, it may destroy you tomorrow. Words have reactions. Actions have reactions.

What are you doing? Are you only caring about you and yours or are you caring about that person out there, whom you do not even know?

Care enough to care. Act selflessly.

* * *
23/Jul/2017 08:17 PM

If you are not basing what you say on saying something positive your words destroy everything.

From your words, your life is born.

*   *   *

23/Jul/2017 08:16 PM

Every day you could do something about it but every day you don't.

Positive Words of Negativity
23/Jul/2017 07:15 AM

When you pick up a book to read have you already decided how you are going to feel about the writing? Though this is a very unenlightened perspective to possess at the outset of any read, some people are like this. This predetermined mindset goes to both sides of the spectrum. There are those who love an author so they believe they will love any book that author composes. Then, on the other side of the coin, there are those who look for a reason to hate a book they have decided to read. They begin their reading experience seeking out a reason to dislike what is written.

But, why is this? Why do people choose to do something with a predetermined perspective? To answer, this really goes to the mindset of the individual. This goes to their psychological makeup. And, it goes to the person they choose to present to the world—even if that person is only presented to family members, close friends, and/or themselves. They want to be seen as a something; a knower.

To ask the question of most people, *"How often have you decided to do something like read a book knowing that you have already made up your mind as to whether or not you will love or hate it?"* For most, the answer would be never. You may end up loving or hating the book but you do not go into the experience of reading it with a mind already made up. It is important to know in life, however, that there are other people out there that want to make something someone else created, *"A something." "A something,"* that they want it to be.

I believe we all remember when we had to write a, *"Book report,"* for a book we were assigned to read in school. In many cases, we were assigned a book that we probably would never have picked up on our own accord. None-the-less, we were given an assignment and we were forced to complete it to the best of our ability. From this, we can all discuss some of the classic works of literature as we were all forced to read and report on a very common list of writings.

Some people enter into reading a book in this manner. They go at it like they are doing a book report. They read it, but instead of allowing it to stand on its own merits to the mind of each individual, they hope to pick it apart and thereby present their personal take on that work as its ultimate authority. Again, why do people do this? The answer to this question is twofold. First of all, this mindset is based in a misplaced sense of being all-knowing. Somehow, someway this person as emerged in their life believing that they possess a deeper sense of understanding than does the average individual and, as such, they tell themselves they have the right to evaluate all things/anything so others will be forced to base their opinion on what they have detailed. The second part of the answer to this equation goes to the individual's level of personal understand of Self in association with the reality of, *"Out there."* Most of these people have found themselves, to whatever degree, shunned by society in the early stages of their life. From this, they have developed a deep sense of insecurity. Though they most likely will never present this insecurity to the world, in fact just the opposite, they live a life of perpetuated judgment based on early life experiences. As they want to overcome this early shunning they step to the forefront of life and present themselves as, *"The knower."* From this, they present what, *"They believe,"* to the world.

The thing about life is that many people do not have a strong, highly developed sense of Self. They want to be part of the crowd. Thus, the people who put themselves at the apex of knowledge easily find followers.

It is very important in life that each of us studies what we are doing, our motivations for what we are doing, and what effect what we are doing is having upon the world. If you enter into anything with predetermined notions, then you are robbing yourself of a true and natural experience for what you are doing in life. If you attach your judgment to what you have previously chosen to encountering than you are taking, *"Choice,"* away from the person listening to what you have to say. If you do this, not only do you become karmiclly responsibly for what happens next in the life of that person who listens to you, but you rob the freedom of choice that the greater whole of the world should be allowed to posses.

      Allow yourself to enter each new experiences with a sense of undefined wonderment and lack of judgment. When you have passed through that experience don't attempt to make others feel the same way as you feel about it. Allow each person to experience life from their own personal perspective. Then, we are each allowed to be who we can ultimately become and each person is allowed to feel the way they want to feel.

* * *
22/Jul/2017 09:08 PM

Just because it is hidden does not mean that it doesn't exist.

* * *
22/Jul/2017 07:40 AM

Do you consciously try to become a better person?

Fight the Good Fight
22/Jul/2017 06:54 AM

There is the age-old statement, *"Fight the good fight."* As all statements can be, this statement can be interpreted in several different ways. But, at its heart, most interpret it as, fighting for what is good and what is right. But, what is good and right? Is good and right a whole thing onto itself or is simply what you believe is good and right?

If you look around at the world, your society, your group of friends, or even at yourself, what do people believe is good? If you study this, you will see that each person, each group, each society, defines good as something different. Yes, there may be large groups of people who come together under one banner to fight for a cause they believe is good and right but look across the street and there will be another group fighting for just the opposite cause. From this, we can understand that, *"Fighting the good fight,"* is a concept based upon personal interpretation and it is not a universal truth.

Think about the things you are passionate about—the things that you believe are right and the things that you believe are wrong. Is there a commonality of those things? That commonality is most likely that they get your juices flowing. This or that makes you angry so first it causes a mental reaction in you which then possibly leads to a physical reaction.

Now, think about the last time you watched on TV as a large group of people destroyed things on a college campus, rioted in a city, beat someone up on the street because someone believed something different than they did, possessed a differing ethnic makeup, or killed people in war. Did all of these people believe that they were fighting the good fight? Probably. But, what that thought did was to cause them do something very negative which can and should never be defined by the word, *"Good,"* on any level.

They were fighting their fight but the minute they entered the world of causing harm, all goodness of their deed was lost.

Look around yourself and the people you interact with on the personal level: at your school, place of employment, at the gym, or on the internet. Is there a commonality of cause that exists between you? What is that commonality? Is it based on someone or something you love or someone or something you hate? If it is based on that ladder what are you are invoking, due to your cause, is negativity. And negativity is always universally based upon personal judgment being cast out the to the world. From this, nothing positive is ever born.

Moreover, is there one person, one personality who draws you and your group together. If so, what you have entered into is a cult of personality. And, a cult of personality has been the sourcepoint for all of the bad things that have happened in the world due to people falling in with a cult.

To define whether or not you are falling in with a cult of personality, take a look at what you say and what you do within the confines of your group. Are you praising one person? Are you saying things that you hope will find you favor with that one person or with your group because you said that positive thing about that one person? If so, you are in a cult of personality and you may be karmically falling prey to any negative deeds that are being unleashed onto individual people and/or the world emanating from that cult.

Fighting the good fight should never be based solely on an emotion filled reaction unleashed onto people or the world. The good fight should be based upon a universally positive reaction to all things in the sphere of life.

We all know, we have all witnessed what saying or doing negative things does to a person, a formulated group, or to a society. If you become part of that negative experience, though it may get your juices flowing, what does it do to the whole of your life? What will it do to you and your ultimate evolution?

Look at your life. Look at what you say and what you do. Look at why you say what you say and do what you do. Look at how you behave towards other people based upon what you feel.

Why do you feel what you feel? Is it a natural realization on your own part? Or, did someone guide you in the direction of feeling what you feel? And, are you feeling what you are feeling to make someone else happy?

At the heart of the, *"Good fight,"* is always the word, *"Good."* Good is always good. There is never anything negative attached to that definition. Do good.

* * *
21/Jul/2017 01:03 PM

If you've judge somebody, you've judge somebody.

If you've said something negative about somebody, you've said something negative about somebody.

What are the consequence both seen and unseen?

If you've accept a person for who and what they are, you've accepted a person for who and what they are.

If you've said something positive about somebody, you've said something positive about somebody.

What are the consequence both seen and unseen?

How would you be judged if you reveled the true you?

What would people say about you if they knew the true you?

The Things That Make You Upset
21/Jul/2017 07:12 AM

For each of us there are situations that occur in our lives that make us upset. For most people, these situations are motivated by something some person has done. …They did something, we didn't like what they did, thus we are upset. But, this is not always the case, some people look outside of themselves and their own life situation to find a reason to be upset. This is not based upon interpersonal relationships, however, it is, in fact, a psychological abnormality. But, no matter what the cause, when an individual is upset this is the time when they are most likely to do something that not only negatively affects the life of the person that has made them upset but their own life, as well.

Look at yourself. Who or what upsets you? Think about a time when you were upset at a person. What was the reason? Most likely, it was due to the fact that they did something that you did not like. But, now look deeper into the situation. Why did they do it? What element of you, your desires, your life, what you previously had done to them, caused them to do what they did to you that ultimately upset you?

If we actually take the time to study our life we will find that, in many cases, the reason we have become upset at a person is actually based in something we instigated. Certainly, most people are not self-aware enough to acknowledge this fact. They forever want to shift the blame onto anyone but themselves. But, the truth be told, in many cases the reason you are upset at a person is because of a situation that was brought into existence by you.

If you can own this fact, not only will you pass through life being far less upset but you will also come to understand human consciousness from a much more refined perspective.

It is not only people that upset us. Sometimes we are mad at the world around us. Maybe you don't like the current political condition of the country where you live, maybe you are mad at the powers-that-be who dominate your life, or maybe you are just frustrated with where you find yourself in life. No matter what the cause, when you are upset at something outside of yourself, that is anger based in a choice. You have decided that you don't like that something. Thus, it causes you to be upset.

The problem with focusing your anger on something, *"Out There,"* is, *"Out There,"* is not, *"In Here."* It is not something that you are. It is something that is pulling you away from yourself and your own personal inner-development.

As I often discuss, anger is an addictive emotion. It is also an extremely negative emotion as it has the potential to make people do some very-very bad things. If you are allowing yourself to have your anger motived by the, *"Out There,"* it takes away from what you are doing towards your own personal development. In fact, that is why so many people focus their mind on the, *"Out There."* They do that so they do not have to look inside themselves, perhaps resolve their own inner issues, and, thereby, come to a new and deeper understanding of their own human consciousness.

We each get dragged into the mindset of being upset from time-to-time. This is simply part of the human condition. This, *"Being upset,"* is generally brought about by the actions of another. Again, this is part of the human condition as most people do not take the time to think about what effect they are having on another person or another person's person life by the words they are speaking or the actions they are unleashing. …People are a selfish breed… This being said, each time you find yourself being upset you can choose to control this emotion as opposed to letting it control you. The fact is, the more times you allow yourself to become upset, at people and situations, as you pass thorough life, the deeper you will allow that emotion to carve its way into your psyche. This is where the addition to being upset is born.

Think about it, do you like to be upset? If you do, you are following a path of aberrant reality. If you don't, teach yourself to not let it control your life.

In closing, I can tell you a funny/interesting story about being upset. Many people believe that spiritual communities, especially those following an Eastern path to realization, are never burdened by people who are angry or upset. This, however, is not universally the case.

When I first found my way to Swami Satchidanand's Integral Yoga Institute, when I was a teenager, I knocked on the door and they invited me in. The female Swami who opened the door had been sitting on the floor putting together a newsletter. With my young mind focused on Karma Yoga (Selfless Service) I happily sat down and began to help her. A few minutes later another female Swami came in and said something to her. The Swami I was initially sitting with got up and walked into the other room where the pair began a big argument. Me, I awkwardly sat there finishing up the newsletter as the two argued in the other room upset at one another about something. There I was, a person they did not yet even know, and there they were, two Swamis, arguing in the other room. I finished up the newsletter and waited for my new friend to return. ☺

You see, people get upset everywhere. But, it is always what you choose to do with that emotion that defines you as a human being.

Killed By Death
20/Jul/2017 12:54 PM

If I can reference the great Motorhead song, *"Killed By Death,"* I think it is very sad that recently it seems there have been a number of seminal artists taking their own life. It was just revealed that Chester Bennington took his own life today. Just a few weeks ago, Chris Cornell also hanged himself. I mean both of these guys had phenomenal voices. And, Chris Cornell truly helped to usher in a new genre of music, Grunge. Sad…

I just heard on TMZ Live that the two were close friends and today would have been Chris Cornell's birthday. So, Bennington was sending some sort of message. He hanged himself at his home very close to where I live. Sad!

Certainly, suicide is nothing new. It has been going on since the dawn of humanity. And, from a philosophic perspective, people should have the right to end their own life if they no longer wish to live. I mean, we do not have a choice about being born but, if we wish, we should have a choice in our death. Though this is usually not the case… Most people when they come up against the door of death, they do not want to enter. Yet, they are pushed through. But, that is getting off the subject.

I think it was probably brought clearly home when Robin Williams took his own life in 2014. In all of these three cases, it appeared as if these people had the world by the tail. …Chris Cornell had just gotten off stage… But, they each chose to get off of the ride.

There is always the discussion after a person takes their own life as to why. Many reference depression, the wrong medications, bullying, a bad breakup, financial crisis, no hope on the horizon, and the list goes on… But, what occurred, for whatever reason, is a person decided they no longer wished to live.

Now, the three aforementioned people were each very famous in their own right. They seemed to be living a very good life. …A life that many of us can only dream of. But, think about all of the people whom you never heard of, who were never famous, and they took their own life, as well. As you didn't know them, never heard of them, do you even care? And, do the fans of these famous people, who take their lives, truly care? Does anyone care about anybody that they do not personally know? And, maybe this goes to the source of the problem… Most people don't care unless they have a reason to care. Maybe that reason is bloodline, maybe it is love, maybe it is money, but if you only possess the ability to care about someone who does something for you, that is doing business that is not a true, deep, interpersonal relationship. Maybe that was what was lacking from their lives of these people—all the people who take their own life. In most cases, we will never know.

But, the one thing to think about as you pass through your life is that you really need to take the full-on focus of your mind off of yourself: what you want, what you think you need, what you think you deserve. You really need think about other people—not just the people you love or those who pay your rent, you need to think about the everybody—the person out there who needs your help—the person whose life that would become so much better if you simply said a kind word to them or did a good deed for them. Think about them. Stop thinking only about yourself. You never know, maybe by behaving in this manner, you will save a person from suicide.

* * *
20/Jul/2017 12:09 PM

There is no way to live in the dirt and not get dirty.

* * *
20/Jul/2017 12:08 PM

I understand that everyone wants everything for free these day. But, if you were the creator of those things you would have a different perspective.

Do you get paid for what you do? Would you do what you do for free?

If You Want Me to Be in the Conversation Let Me Be in the Conversation
20/Jul/2017 06:38 AM

Whenever I create a narrative-driven film I allow my actors to speak the way they would naturally speak—say what they would naturally say. From this, I believe it provides their character with a sense of realism.

In times gone past, Donald G. Jackson and I would feed our characters their lines in our Zen Films. But, I left that ideology behind long ago, as it is not as real as real.

In my Zen Films, what I do is allow the actors to say whatever they want. I give them a bit of framework for their character at the outset and then I let them run with it. The only time I interrupt is if they are going totally off storyline. Then, I leave it to the editing room to find the best of the best. That's the great thing about cinema, you have time. It's not like TV that has to be cut down to a very precise period of time. The filmmaker has freedom, if they allow themselves to embrace it. Thus, I want my actors to be a part of this process of cinematic freedom.

When it comes to life, I also think this is the best practice—let people say what they will say. From this, you are allowed to see into their psychic; as what they say and the way they say it can provide you with deep insight into how they truly feel about you, life, and themselves. What a person chooses to say and how they choose to say it is very revealing about who they truly are on the inside.

As an actor, on the sets of other director's films, in many cases, I have been given a script with lines to memorizes. That's fine but is that person me? No, it is a person I am pretending to be. In some cases, in small parts in A-Films, I have been given an on-set line or two to speak. But, I always find those words are forced and predictable. How often do you only say one line? I always felt if they wanted me to speak, they should let me speak. Then, like in the case of Zen Filmmaking, a natural conversation would evolve. From this, the audience would be treated to a condition of naturalness.

The one exception to this was the film I did directed by Robert Altman, *The Player*. I arrived on the set to play the role of, *"White Guy."* Yes, in all truth that is what my character's name was given in the actual script. I still have the original script so I can prove it! In that case, as we begin to shoot second part for my character on the stairwell of the Rialto Theater in Pasadena, I didn't like the line that had been written for me. I told this to Bob. He said, say whatever you want. *"You got the wrong guy, man."* From this, it caused a moment of reflection in the film. I remember being at the premier of, *The Player*. With great cinema creation and story development, the filmmaking team had built my charterer up to the degree that after my character's set up in the movie theater, watching the movie the Bicycle Thief, the audience all gasp when I said that simple line. And, as the person who created it, that was a really good feeling!

Most of the time on the set, the actors don't have that freedom, however. They are forced to speak words that have been memorized from a script. This is just like in life; you are trapped in an environment where you must be defined by what you are defined by. Thus, you are not allowed to say what you actually feel. This is why the internet has taken off to the degree that it has—anyone can say anything thing. And, hidden by a screen name, no one knows who you truly are, so they can't confront you face-to-face about what you have said—thus there is a veil of protection.

Yeah, yeah… This is the coward's way out. I agree! But, for all those with no voice, here they have a voice.

But, more to the point, think about when you speak to people… Do the people you know, (the people you actually associate with in real life), allow you to speak in the manner you truly desire? Moreover, do they hear you? Do they listen to what you have to say, consider your point of view, and perhaps change their mind to give your point of view room to grow in life?

Truthfully, most people's lives are not like that. Most people do not want you to speak. If you do speak, most people do not want to listen to what you have to say. At best, they pay you lip service and then continue on their path of self-induced righteous.

Life is a complicated pathway. As I bought up the internet, I can say, there is no true dialogue out here. No one says they're sorry, because no one care about the consequences. At least they don't care about the consequences to others—only themselves. But, this is a shallow place to live your life from for at the end of the day what will it equal? Only you saying what you said, somebody else saying what they said, but no interaction and growing of the minds of multiple people. Thus, evolution is halted. There is only you and no one else.

So, back to the original point, if you want me to be in the conversation, let me be in the conversation. Just like an actor in a film, let me speak in a natural way. Then, you will know me, I will know you, and we can create a new evolution of life and understanding.

No New Converts
19/Jul/2017 07:06 AM

How many people have you known in your life that have changed? How many people have you actually known that have perhaps heard some inspirational words, read an inspiring book, or maybe had a realization, and then have changed? …Have stopped living their life from a selfish perspective, thinking only about themselves, and set about on a course of doing and saying only good things, actually helping people, and consciously attempting to make the world a better more spiritual place? My guess would be none.

The people who consciously walk the path of consciousness are few. Most who do acquire this inclination when they are very young. But, there have been others who have had their life shaken up, generally by some tragedy, and then have changed—they are forced into a new understanding of life awareness and from that realization they move forward with a conscious inclination to do good things, to help people, and to attempt to make all things better. But, these people are few.

Look around yourself—look at the people you know, how many of them care? Some may be nice, some may be funny, some may even be religious; but how many of them actually make the conscious choice to get out there and make the world a better place?

Certainly, it can be argued that the people who are on the forefront of helping others do so to gain a sense of accomplishment. From a psychological perspective, this may well be the case. But, think about the effect they are having on the world compared to that of the person who thinks about nothing but themselves: what they like, what they dislike, what they want, and whom they wish to become. Which person do you believe makes the greater contribution to the world and to human society?

When you wake up in the morning what do you think about? Here, is the ideal place to chart where your consciousness lies. For parents, many wake up thinking about their children. This is a good and natural first-thought. For young lovers, they may wake up thinking about the person lying next to them. Again, that is natural. But, to the greater whole, when you wake up in the morning what is your first thought? Is your first thought about you or is it about what you can do for the betterment of all? Is it you thinking, *"I need a cup of coffee?"* Or, is it you thinking, *"Today I am going to do this particular something to try to make that person's life a little better?"*

The truth be told, no matter what you say to the person who only thinks about themselves, they are not going to change their mind. This is why there are no new converts. This is why so much of the world's populous goes around hurting each other. People only think about themselves.

This is being said, it can be you who actually chooses to make the change—chooses to be more and do more. You personally; you can make the world a better place. How do you do this? By caring about others instead of only caring about yourself.

The Last Laugh
18/Jul/2017 01:14 PM

I just had a chance to check out the first preview for James Franco's upcoming movie, *The Disaster Artist.* The movie is based on the making of Tommy Wiseau's film, *The Room.* I have never met Tommy nor have I seen his film, *The Room.* But I have, of course, heard about him and the film. I have to say it must feel pretty good for Tommy to have the last laugh. I mean all of those people who have talked shit about him, particularly on the internet, and now Big-Dollar Hollywood is making a Bio Pic about him with a cast made up of A-List talent. That must feel pretty good!

I had a very small example of that happen to me about ten years ago when a group of students at Grand Valley State University in Michigan made a ten-part mockumentary goofing on me, Don, and Zen Filmmaking. I just found it one day on YouTube. I have mentioned this here in this blog before but you can get to it by going to my YouTube channel or by searching Zen Filmmaking on YouTube. It was a great piece of true Zen Filmmaking. I never met any of those people. If you are out there you should get in touch with me and we can make a Zen Film together. I'll bring the camera. ☺

But, that was a small budget project. Nothing like, Wiseau. He gets the big bank behind him. That's great! It's a true testament to indie filmmakers who make less than mainstream presentations.

It must have been an interesting experience for him to work with those people on that level. I know whenever I'm called up to The Bigs it is a trip. I mean the amount of people and the amount of money they spend on those big productions. It is scary. I think I've mentioned this before, in some previous blog (somewhere), but on the last A-Market film I did they had this stand-in for my character. It was funny. He was the much younger, better looking, version of me. I told him, he should be the one in front the camera. Though most of my part ended up on the cutting room floor—but that's okay, it's not all that unusual as the big films shoot so much footage that is never used it is scary. Like I tell my actor friends when they complain about that kind of thing happening to them, *"You should be really thankful! They treat you like a king (or queen), you get paid stupid amounts of money, and you don't have to do anything to earn it."*

I checked Tommy's IMDB.com page and it doesn't look like he has made a full fledged movie like, *The Room,* since 2003. But, I guess that's all he needed to do. It was enough to get the attention of Hollywood and have James Franco play him in a film. Congratulations to all concerned!

Right Thought and What You Do Today Equals Your Tomorrow
18/Jul/2017 06:37 AM

As I often discuss in this blog, the world is created by you. What you do today sets your tomorrow into motion. What you say or do spreads from you and has the potential to affect the entire world. Thus, you must be very focused on what you say and what you do if you hope for not only your own life to be lived as a good life but for all you encounter to have a positive experience. This is why one of the key concepts to Buddhist philosophy is the understanding of, *"Right Thought."*

Take a moment and look at your life. Think about a time when you were angry, jealous, mad, envious, greedy, or lust driven. How did that make you feel? Now, look deeper into that time in your life—more than simply how you felt what did that emotion cause you to say or do? And, what was the result of what you said or did?

If we look outside of ourselves, we can easily see how anger has caused many people to do very-very bad things. Even if they did not actually intend to do something bad, they were emotion driven and bad results occurred.

In many ways, it is easy to critique the life of someone else, it is much harder for you to look at yourself and to truly view what a negative emotion has caused you to do and what were its wide spanning consequences. The reason for this is simple, most people believe that what they are feeling is right and they have a reason for feeling the way they are feeling. Thus, any outburst or action they unleash they feel is justified. But, is it? Is what you think and feel more important than what another person thinks and feels? Some will immediately answer, *"Yes, it is."* But, that is a selfish mindset speaking. A True Person always considers another person before they speak and/or act.

Let's look at the source of emotional action a little bit further. Remember a time when you were feeling a certain way and that emotion caused you act. You acted, you did what you did, you affected the life of another person the way you affected the life of another person but what was the ultimate benefit to you? Did it all of a sudden make your entire life better? Maybe you felt good for a moment for getting over on another person that you were angry at or did not like, but did that action truly make your overall life any better? Moreover, what were the long term ramifications of your action? If you hurt somebody, now they are probably angry at you. Now what? Do you need to look over your shoulder?

The problem with Self-Though and only thinking about yourself—only being driven by what you are feeling in a particular moment is that it does not lead to a better ALL in your life. Plus, basing your life on the temporality of emotion is that you create a lot of karma for yourself. And, though in one moment you may be flush with friends cheering you on, in the long term any negative action based upon any negative thought or emotions comes back to take its toll on your life. Thus, this is why the Buddhist practices, *"Right Thought."*

What is Right Thought? Just as the combination of words imply, it is thinking righteous thoughts. It is controlling your thoughts so your thoughts do not control you. It is causing yourself to not be controlled by your emotions so that you do not do bad things that hurt other people which will ultimately hurt you.

Right Thought is not necessarily easy if you have lived a life defined by uncontrolled emotions. Though it is not necessarily easy, it is the easiest thing to do. Just get control of yourself! Just get control over your mind! Don't let your emotions dominate your every thought causing you to unleash selfish, uncaring actions.

By taking control, you are in control. By being in control, that will give you a thousand times more internal pleasure than you would gain from constantly being in a state of disharmony brought about by your own lack of self-projected fulfillment.

And, this is the main point... Why are you ever angry, jealous, or greedy? Because you are unfulfilled. Why are you unfulfilled? Because you want more and/or you want control. You want all that you want when you want it. But think about this... What if you just let go of that anger? What if you just let go of that jealousy? What if you just let go of that desire? Think how free you would be. Think how happy you would become. And, from this, no negative action would be born based upon you doing negative things based upon a negative emotion.

Be free. Think Right Thoughts.

Never the Same
17/Jul/2017 02:19 PM

In everyone's life things happen that change everything forever. Some of these events are very small while others are very large, most fall somewhere in between. The one thing they all have in common is that they are memorable and life altering enough that your life is never the same once they occur.

Yesterday, a guy ran into my lady's car as we were driving home from celebrating National Ice Cream Day at a local ice cream shop. All was well with the world but the guy, looking at his phone, didn't see that we were stopped at a light and smashed into her car and the impact then shoved it into the SUV in front of us. Her car is totaled. Though it was fairly old but it ran well and she liked it, so what more can you ask. But, it's gone... Now, we have to deal with all of the nonsense of getting her another car. The paramedics showed up and wanted to take me to the hospitable but I, of course, turned that down. My neck's a little tweaked but hopefully it will get better. So, there it is, an example of a relatively small event that changes everything forever.

Certainly, I've had far worse accidents, like when a girl, driving her Mercedes, ran into my motorcycle when I was twenty-one almost killing me. Nothing about my life was ever the same... But, does she even remember or care about what she did?

This goes to the point of what you do, why you do it, and how you do it. There are enough accidents in life that can change your everything forever, why should you set about on a course and consciously do anything that will alter anybody's life? What makes you think you have the right?

Some people are very conscious of other people. They truly care about adding to the greater good. They are good people and try to only do good things. On the other hand, some people are flat-out bad. They live a life course that hurts others. But, look at their lives over time. Where do they end up? You will see that behaving in that manner will catch up to them.

Most people, however, do not try to be good. They do not try to make the world a better place. Just as most people are not bad, they do not try to hurt or take from others. It is the people in the middle who either live their life from a space of uncaring unconsciousness or possess a misplaced sense of entitlement that causes many of the Never-the-Same crisis to occur in the lives of other people.

I talk about this kind of stuff all the time. I really hope people will think about what they are doing before they do it, chart what effect it may have: whom it will help and whom it will hurt. I believe most of the people who reads this blog are like that. They do not want to be the cause of creating Never-the-Same moments in people's lives unless it is based on the case of making someone's life better. But, there are all those others out there who do not care enough to care. They only think about themselves: they justify their actions and surround themselves with people who are telling them they are okay. But, hurting anyone is never okay. Don't support people who live their life from that frame of mind. This is why you really must become WHOLE enough in yourself to study what you are doing before you do it. Care enough to care! If it is going to hurt someone/anyone don't do it. If you do hurt someone, at least be like they guy who ran into my lady's car yesterday and be adult enough to apologize like he did, be calm, and try to make things better. As better is always better!

There are enough uncharitable accidents in this world that will cause people to be Never-the-Same. Don't consciously do anything that causes that catastrophe in anyone's life.

The Harsh Realms of Reality
16/Jul/2017 03:19 PM

I always find it curious the way people focus on so much outside of themselves. They think and talk about all the things in life that do not truly affect them. Yet, they form opinions and discuss what they think about this person or that, that organization or this, what they would do if and when they could, they discuss how someone else should live and what others should do. But, none of this adds up to anything but the sheer rambling meaninglessness of life. It does not equal anything! Yet, how many people focus their entire life upon this style of banter.

I should say, that people behave in this manner only when they are allowed to do so. …Only when they are living a life of safety and wholeness; where they have enough to eat, a safe place to live, and do not have to fight a war every time that they walk out the front door.

Think about it, there are a lot of people who must live their life at that level. I imagine if you are reading this blog you do not… And, that is a good thing… But, on the other side of the issue, do you live your life based on the concept of privilege? And, do you ever consider what you are doing, how you are living your life, and why? Do you ever consider the big picture before you say what you say and/or do what you do? Do you ever view the reality of your life, what you are creating with your life, based upon where you find yourself in life? If you don't you should.

* * *

15/Jul/2017 12:36 PM

When you do not know the facts, your opinion has no validity.

Loving the Melodrama
15/Jul/2017 08:29 AM

Some people love melodrama in their life. They are constantly looking for something to make them excited, angry, dissatisfied—all in order to get that rush that comes from that burst of adrenaline based upon an intense emotion. For these people, if they cannot automatically find something to stir their juices they create it. I have known several people who live their life based upon this mindset.

Personally, I don't like that feeling. I don't like to feel angry, nervous, paranoid, or enraged. So me, I don't look for things to stir those emotions. When they have come to my life it is usually by the hands of one of those people who likes that kind of stuff and as they use whatever method necessary to get their emotional fix they oftentimes drag others into their melodrama.

Has that as that ever happened to you? Has anyone ever created a situation where you were dragged into a melodramatic situation by the words or the action of another person? How did you feel about that? And, have you ever done that to another person? Have you ever done something that brought disruption and chaos to the life of another person? Why did you do it?

Certainly, in the real realms of life is where these emotions take hold but online I always find it an interesting place to observe human behavior. It is quite easy to view how people behave in life by the websites they visit, by the screen names they choose, by the words they choose to write on those sites, and especially by the way they describe and interact with others. I mean look around the various sites online where they allow people to express their opinions and you will easily be able to see how some people are positive, passive, nice, and understanding, while others are like attack dogs—what they say and do is based upon a defined sense of personal judgment and anger being expressed from the mindset of I am right, you are wrong; I hate you.

Each person's life is made up by the experiences they experience as they pass through life. Each person's life is also defined by the experiences they create in their own life and the ones they instigate in the lives of other people. This is where karma is born.

How many people do you know who live their life on the level of existence where they draw others into their realm of emotion-driven consciousness and do so from a place of caring or understanding? Almost universally you will find that people who create melodrama, (and draw others into it), do so from a very personally undefined since of reality where they are not in touch with themselves, they do not truly care about anyone but themselves, and they do not care what effect they are having on the lives of others—they only care about seeking their emotional rush.

We each have a choice how we encounter life. We also have a choice of what we bring to the lives of others by what we say and what we do. How is what you are saying and doing affecting your life and, in may ways more importantly, how is what you are saying and doing affecting the lives of other people? And, do you care about any of this? If you don't, that is the perfect description of you as a human being. Do you like that person?

In life, unless we hide from the world, we each are going to encounter undesired melodrama in life—even if we are one of the people who does not seek it out. Almost universally this will be brought to our life by another person who is either questing this type of mental stimulation, (via either a conscious or unconscious method), or by someone who simply is unconscious of their actions or does not even care enough to care. But, it is what you do with that energy when it attacks you that defines you as a human being. We can allow ourselves to be dragged into the negativity of it or we we can sidestep the attack, remain conscious, and hold tight to our Best Self while the turbulent energy surges around us.

We are all here in life together. Some hope to make each person's life better while others only think about themselves. This has been the definition of life since the beginning of time. All you can do is make the best, most positive decisions available to you when you are confronted by the random mind games of another.

Be strong. Be positive. Care about others. Think about the effect of what you are doing will have on others. Live a good life. Create a good life for other people.

*   *   *
14/Jul/2017 01:34 PM

Do you ever watch the news or the online news feeds and see all of the bad things that are taking place in the world?

What is the common denominator of these bad deeds?

It is people doing things that hurt other people.

Do you participate in any of those bad deeds?

Do you make excuses or provide justifications for your words or your actions?

Small things grow to equal big things.

If anyone is hurt by what you say or what you do you are performing a negative action that leads to a bad deed being performed.

As you are the sourcepoint, you are responsible for all that happens in the world.

Study what you say and what you do. See where your words and your actions lead and what they lead to.

Make the world a safer, better place.

Old Enough to Be Your Grandfather
14/Jul/2017 07:15 AM

I had kind of a funny/interesting experience the other day. I got talking to one of my barista buddies at Starbucks. I was surprised to find out that, for some reason, he thought I was around the same age as him, mid-thirties. He didn't believe me when I told him how old I am. *"You want to see my ID,"* I joking exclaimed. *"I'm old enough to be your father!"*

I guess I am lucky in that I haven't gone very grey as of yet. But, I am sure it will catch up with me sooner rather than later. And yes, the functionality of my body has been destroyed by my five plus decades of doing the martial arts. But overall, I feel pretty good.

That being said, I would imagine that most of the people who read this blog are of the age that they could be my children or even grandchildren. Inside, that makes me laugh. I'm old! Even though I feel very young.

Aging as never bothered me. Some people run away from it, lie about their age, get plastic surgery, dye their hair, and do all that kind of stuff. Not me. I embrace it.

And, this brings us to the point of all this rambling…

From age, it gives you the time to watch things change and to observe the trends and the patterns of people. For lack of a better phrase, yes, it does give you wisdom if you are aware enough to observe life.

When you were growing up maybe you were told to, *"Respect your elders."* I know I was. Certainly, as I have been highly interactive with Asian culture throughout most of my life I have observed how, even if a person does not like one of their older family or group members they pay them respect. But here, in the Western world, everyone is so self-empowered they pay no tribute to anything, they show no respect to anyone for any reason. They don't care about the fact that maybe they are wrong, just if they can scream the loudest to make themselves seem right. They do this to anyone, everyone, no matter what their age or what their status in life. But, I believe that something is lost for those who embrace this mindset.

I watched in the 1960s how it became taboo to be old. *"Don't trust anyone over thirty,"* was one of the mottos. The 60s, of course, was a time of rapid cultural change. This change was seemingly orchestrated by the thoughts and actions of the young. Thus, age became a detriment.

The thing about youth verse age, however, is think about those youth from the 1960s, how old are the now? Or, are they even still alive?

Time is the master of us all. We all pass through life. If we live long enough we all become old. But, it is what you with your time here in life, as you pass from youth to old, that is what defines you as a person and, in fact, defines your lasting effect on this Life-Place.

The thing about our current time is that so many people, (especially the young), live their life on the internet, staring at a screen. Though this is certainly the name of the game of the current era, there is something very false and disingenuous about this. No one is anybody. They are a screen name which is something that is non-existent. They rarely, if ever, bridge that gap between cyber space and reality with the people they communicate with or talk about. Thus, their reality is not real—meaning they are not real. In the Hindu and Buddhist concept of Maya, (that life is illusion), this is the ultimate example.

The thing is, via personal interaction and personal communication, a person comes to truly understand another individual. I believe we have all had the experience where we have emailed somebody something, that we have written, and the other person took it totally the wrong way. The written words didn't truly convey our intended meaning. This is the perfect example because if the personal communication had been face-to-face then the intent of the words would have been correctly understood. …As you can read the facial and body language of a person and hear the way their words are spoken.

But, more to the point… From personal interaction, you have the opportunity to come to understand a person on a much more subtle level. If you are of the same age group, you may have common life experiences. If someone is younger, you can witness that you may have encountered certain life experiences that this person is yet to meet. And, if you personally speak with someone who is older, you may realize that they have gone through life events that you have not. From this, you may be able to learn something from them and avoid some of the life obstacles they have encountered.

Youth to age is the established pattern of life. There is no way around it. What I believe people need to do is to come to a deeper understanding of this process, instead of demeaning or running away from it, and take the time to listen to those who have walked the path before you as they probably have a lot to teach. I know I have done this throughout my life and even if I did not ultimately agree with the person, I was always able to learn something about life from them.

Tick Tock. You're getting old!

Not A Chinaman's Chance
13/Jul/2017 07:56 PM

I spend a lot of my free time watching and studying old movies. My preference lies to late 1930s and 1940s cinema but in reality I love cinema from all eras. In fact, I've been asked to write a book on midcentury cinema a couple of times. But, I have, at least so-far, turned all those offers down. Having read far too many poorly researched and/or written books, I just have not wanted to add to that literary concoction.

The one thing I find in older cinema is how it truly depicts the mindset of the era. The way people speak, especially when they speak in slang, truly allows one to reference and understand how people understood and transmitted the culture of that time period. Certainly, what is allowed to be said verse what is not allowed to be said, lets one peer into the culture of the period. Whereas cussing in all shapes and sizes is simply thought to be the norm in current cinema, that was not the case it times gone past where there was virtually no, *"Bad language,"* used in films.

On the other side of the coin, what has become the modern culture of, *"Political correctness,"* in today's film marketplace, was not at all the case in times gone past. I was watching a movie from the 1930s today and they used the expression, *"Not a Chinaman's Chance,"* meaning that there was little or no chance of it happening. Can you imagine the uproar if someone made that statement in a modern film? It would be called racist. Again, this goes to the mindset of the era.

In today's society, what one says and how they say it must be highly calculated so no one, of any specific ethnic group, will be offended. But, looking back, this was not even a thought. Look to the war era films where it was commonplace to refer to Germans as, *"Krauts,"* or the Japanese as, *"Nips."*

We, as a universal people on this planet have evolved, and that evolution is revealed in the way we speak in films. In fact, this can be seen represented throughout human history. If you look back, just a couple of centuries, virtually no one travelled anywhere. Travel was very-very limited. From this came a homogenous culture where everyone saw anyone, even if from just a few miles away, as a stranger to be feared. As we as humans have moved from the industrial to the technological age, travel has become more and more common. From this, people have witnessed and embraced the traits of other cultures. Though obviously sometimes this intercultural mixation is and has not been an easy one. None-the-less, it is happening. So much so that soon there will be one race.

With cinema as a representation of cultural, we can witness this in the ways racially sensitive terms that were once used in abundances have diminished drastically. This observable quality in itself, is another clue to how cinema portrays the culture of when it was created.

Cinema has certainly overtaken novels as a means of fictionally portraying culture and spreading it from generation to generation. With the widespread dissemination of cinema, from all eras, now on the internet, this will continue to be the case. All this being said, if you take the time to study the words used and the way the actors spoke them, in each era of cinema, you can truly peer back into your culture and define the point in time where actual cultural transformation took place.

Who Do the Gods Pray To?
13/Jul/2017 05:03 PM

I go to this Hindu temple sometimes. It is really a very elaborate, beautiful place. It is highly ornamented.

In India, it is not unusual to find temples of this caliber. But, here in the States, there are only a very-very few. This one being one of the nicest.

When I go there, I am generally the only non-South Asian person inside its walls. I guess not too many Caucasian find their spiritual sustenance in this religion. Though all of those in attendance are of South Asian descent, I never feel anything but welcomed.

The last time I was there, I was taking my shoes off at the base of the stairs to the entrance. For those of you who may not know, you never wear your shoes inside a Hindu temple. Generally, first you take your shoes off, then you wash your feet before you go inside. I won't go into all of the hygienic and symbolic reasons for that practice, but it is what is done. As I was taking my shoes off, I got into a small conversation with another devotee. He was a medical doctor still wearing his scrubs. Nice, friend guy.

Eventually, I made my way inside and spent a few moments, as I like to do, just absorbing the spiritual energy before I do anything else. As I stood there, I notice that the aforementioned doctor was in full prostration, (laying completely down on the ground, face first). To Westerners, this practice may seem strange. But, to the truly devoted Hindu, it is not uncommon at all.

What I was seeing caused me to think… As I am in close association with several people in the medical profession and a few medical doctors, I have come to know how their brains works. In some cases, these people feel all-empowered. I have heard them described, (especially the surgeons), as possessing the god complex. Yet, here he was, a man that held the key to life and death in his hands in full prostration to the gods.

I think few people possess that devotion. And, I believe that is sad, for so much of the world's problems are caused by people who think they have the right to do anything they want to do, yet, they possess none of the skillset of this doctor who was completely devoted to his god. More people should be like him.

* * *

13/Jul/2017 11:32 AM

If you want to say something negative you can always find someone to listen to you.

If you are saying something positive, that is a different story.

Caring About People
13/Jul/2017 06:05 AM

Have you ever been sitting in a restaurant or some public place like that and you look around and take a conscious notice of the people around you? Do you ever study them? Do you ever wonder how they got to where they are in life and why? And, do you care? Do you/can you care about them? Can you care about that person as a human being?

Think about this, there you are in a restaurant… Maybe you're sitting there by yourself. What are you thinking about? Are you thinking about how you can help that person at the next table—how you can make their life better? Probably not.

Most people spend all of their lifetime thinking only of themselves and perhaps those they love. This is the human condition. But, it is also a choice. At each moment of your life, you have the opportunity to care enough to care about someone else, their well-being, and perhaps making their life a little bit better, even if it takes effort on your part to do it. Or, you can think only about yourself, what you want, and what will make your life better.

People pursue what they desire in life. Some people are very driven and go after what they want until they get it. In this pursuit, the driven do not care who they hurt or who's life they damage in the process as a long as they get what they want. From this mindset, that person sitting at the table next to you may have been held back from becoming all they could have become in life due to the desire-filled actions of another.

Some people think of others. Perhaps they donate to charities maybe they even do some volunteer work. From this, they may be having a positive effect on the greater whole of what they have given to. And, that is a good thing.

But, the question is, do they care about the person sitting at the table next to them?

When you are face-to-face with somebody, that is reality. If you like the way they look, the way they speak, or the way they behave, caring about them is easy. But, what if it is just the opposite? What if you don't like the way they look or the way they act, can you care about them?

This goes to the concept of judgment. …How each person views another person and places a categorical definition upon them. The problem is, there are so many things that goes into what a person has become in their life and what image they project to the world, that any definition you may place on them is a completely biased appraisal of their life which may or may not be correct.

This brings us back to the question… Like them, dislike them, love them, hate them, can you care about them?

It is a truly holy quality when a person can put their own desires and self-thoughts aside, if even for a moment, and care enough to care about the person sitting next to them. Care, no matter what definition they put on their life.

Caring is a choice. It is a choice you can or cannot make at any moment of your life. You can decide to care about a person: what they are feeling and what they are needing or you can decide to only think about yourself.

Most people will say, caring about others is the greater choice. But, most people do not make that choice. They are driven by what they are feeling and what they are wanting and they do not care about anyone else. But, you can. You can care enough to care. You can make the choice to care. You can make the choice to turn off your desires and do what you can to make the life of the person sitting next to you better.

Caring is a choice. Is it a choice you choose to make?

Life Philosophy in a Nutshell
11/Jul/2017 05:33 PM

Life Philosophy in a Nutshell:

Say only good things. Do only good things. Help everyone you can.

Never judge anyone—their accomplishments or their creations.

Don't tell lies.

Never intentionally hurt anyone for any reason.

If you do hurt someone apologize and do all that you can to repair any damage that you've inflicted.

*   *   *
11/Jul/2017 08:05 AM

When is it too late to turn around?

*   *   *
11/Jul/2017 08:05 AM

A saint in one faith is a sinner in another.

* * *
11/Jul/2017 08:05 AM

You are responsible for all things that you incite.

* * *
11/Jul/2017 08:04 AM

The only reason you think about the past is because you are not content in your present.

* * *
11/Jul/2017 08:03 AM

When the destination no longer exists, there is no right or wrong way to get there.

* * *
11/Jul/2017 08:02 AM

If you expect nothing you will never be disappointed.

Doesn't It Make You Feel Stupid When You Are Wrong?
11/Jul/2017 08:01 AM

Recently, it was brought to my attention that Google is currently using a photograph of one the other Scott Shaw's in association with their main link to my information on their website. They are using a photo of the cartoonist, Scott Shaw! A good guy, but he and I are two very different people. Yet, there it is, out there on the number one search engine in the world. But, they are wrong. That's not me. I don't know why they changed the photograph, they had the right one up there forever? But, Goggle being Google there is no way you can readily get in touch with them and tell them they are wrong. And, would they even care? In fact, on Scott Shaw!'s main page they have him listed as winning the Pulitzer Prize for News Photography. But, he didn't win the Pulitzer Prize. That's the photographer Scott Shaw. There's a lot of us Scott Shaw's out there. ☺

The thing is, many people believe everything that they see and/or read on the internet. First of all, I always question this mindset. Why do people do that? Why do they take everything at face value? Moreover, I wonder why people post stuff when they have no factual basis for their opinions posing as facts? But, the big question is, *"Doesn't it make you feel stupid when you are wrong?"* I mean, how much of what you say is wrong? Where did you get your facts? Why are you speaking what you think you know? What karma does that create in your life when you say something that isn't true? And, what are you going to do about it?

I think back to a girl I was speaking with one time and somehow/somewhere/someway she came to believe that Adolph Hitler was from Australia. When she exclaimed her fact, I smiled and explained to her that she simple didn't hear correctly as he was from Austria. But, she wouldn't believe me. She knew her facts and that was that. But, her facts were wrong. Yet, she fought like crazy to make me believe her.

I wonder how many people she spoke that bogus fact to listened to her and, at least for a moment, believed her? Moreover, I wonder how did she feel when and if she ever discovered that she was wrong?

…Speaking of Scott Shaw! Just a funny side note here… When we created the movie *Lingerie Kickboxer* Kevin Eastman had a great poster drawn by the famed artist Simon Bizley. He then had a thousand copies of the poster run. At that point, we still planned to release the movie and the poster was a predecessor to its release. Anyway, one day I walked into Golden Apple back when it was in its original location in the main section of Melrose Ave. in West Hollywood. I noticed the *Lingerie Kickboxer* poster hanging on the wall over the cash register. It was signed by Kevin and Julie Strain. I asked the guy at the cash register if he wanted me to sign it, as well, as I'm Scott Shaw one of the directors. Hey, my name was on the poster. He said, *"You're not Scott Shaw."* As Golden Apple is a comic book based store the guy assumed it was the other Scott Shaw! who was the co-director. But hey, the title and the original concept for the movie was my idea! Anyway, I laughed it off and told him to check his facts. So, this isn't the first time something like this Scott Shaw thing has happened. ☺…

Ask yourself, *"How much of what you think and believe is based upon proven fact verse how much of what you think and believe is based upon something you heard somewhere from someone speaking something that they simply believed, based upon personal bias or being told a lie by someone who didn't know what they were talking about in the first place?"*

Ask yourself, *"What do you do—how do you behave once you learn that what you believed was false?"* Do you move to rectify your incorrect knowledge and what you have broadcast to the world or do you fight like the aforementioned person to make your false knowledge fact?

As we pass through life, each of us evolves in knowledge and understanding. Some of us seek the truth. Others, simply want to believe what they want to believe and speak all of their words as if they were fact when, at best, they are misplaced speculations.

As we each evolve we each learn at every moment of our life. If you lock yourself into the mindset of believing that you already know, then you can never become the MORE that you could have become. If you do not have the mental aptitude and the caring nature to cancel out any false, opinionated, deceptive knowledge that you have broadcast to others how does that create the projection of you to the world? If you cannot turn off your ego long enough to simply say, *"I was wrong,"* and not attach all kinds of reasonings and justifications to that statement then your new truth will forever be burdened with your pervious lie.

"Doesn't it make you feel stupid when you are wrong?"

Just Another Reason to Make People Look at You
11/Jul/2017 08:00 AM

There is a certain feeling that comes over each of us when we look in the mirror and we like what we are wearing, maybe we like the way our hair is looking, and so we feel pretty good about ourselves. There is the opposite feeling when we have gone outside and we discover that we hate what we are wearing—maybe we have spilled something on our shirt or we catch a glance of our self in a window and we realize we look terrible. These are normal emotions based on the perception of ourselves in association with how we perceive reality.

This is why monks only wear very basic, one colored clothing and either shave their head or do not shave or cut their hair at all. But, the fact is, this too is a perceived projection of reality and a source of ego gratification for once they have donned their monk garb, they have become a, *"Something."* Thus, they are projecting that, *"Something,"* to the world. And, they like what that projection brings to them.

Most people want to be seen as something. They want to project an image of themselves to the world. There are those who love the way they look. There are also those who hate the way they look. In each case, each person works with what they have and either falls prey to their love or their hatred for themselves. We are all defined by what we are given but it is us who decided to do what we do with what we were given.

More than simply a physical issue, people want to project an image of who and what they are to the world via their thoughts and their words. Some people are very loud. They scream to the world, *"Here I am! Look at me! This is what I do! This is what I think!"* Others, are silent.

At the heart of all of this doing is the individual's perception of themselves. No matter what they truly are deep down inside, each person has an idea of who they want to be and how they want to be viewed by others. From this is born a cornucopia of lies, false tales, altered truths, individualized perceptions, projected realities, hopes, and dreams. The words people speak are more often based in how they hope to be perceived by others than any other element in life. Thus, for most, all inner truth is lost and it is replaced by how a person hopes another person will view them.

Think about yourself. How do you dress? You do you wear your hair? Do you care about what you wear? Do you care about how your hair is styled?

What do you do in life? Do you tell people the truth about what you do?

How do you live? Do you tell people the truth about how you live and what you do to give yourself the ability to live?

Do you hide or alter any facts about yourself when you discuss yourself with others?

Taking the focus away from yourself, think about your interactions with other people. Throughout your life have you watched what other people wear, how they style their hair, what they say, how they say it, what they do and how they do it? How has that affected you becoming you?

Moreover, as you have passed through your life, have you ever encountered a person who has deceived you about who and what they truly are? Has anyone lied to you? What effect did that have on your life?

If you do not chart what you are doing and how what you are doing is affecting your life, your life is a life lost to uncalculated occurrences. If you do not analyze what you are doing, why you are doing it, and what affect what you are doing will have on others, your life is lost to a never ending array of karmic reactions motivated by your own lack of self-awareness.

If you only care about yourself and do not consider how what you are doing and why you are doing it will effect one person or the whole world you are living in a space of defined selfishness.

Look at you your life. Look at the people who have lied to you, deceived you, stolen from you, hurt you. Why have they done this? The answer is, selfishness. Is that how you want to behave?

If you want to live a whole life, you need to study and come to a deep understanding of the whole you. You are the source of all you will encounter in your life. Understand this and your life becomes a calculated pathway as opposed to undefined rambling interaction of life shaking events.

Surrounding Yourself with What You Hate
11/Jul/2017 07:59 AM

Most people wish to live a simple, happy life. They hope to be surrounded by people they love and people who love them. They hope to pass through life doing things they like to do. Some even hope to make the world a better place. There is the other side of this mindset, however. There are those of the mind who wish to find things in life that makes them angry. Though they are most likely not aware enough to realize it, they do this seeking to gain the adrenalin rush associated with this emotion based upon the negative emotion of anger.

The problem with pursuing this mindset is, whatever you focus your life upon comes to define your life. It comes to define you. From this, all that you do, based upon this life definition, emanates from you, surrounds you, and ultimately causes you to attract those of like mind. From this, if you live a life focused upon things that you hate, all of your life and lifetime becomes a negative experience defined by negative emotions.

It is easy to see the people who live their life based upon what they hate. They are the ones who are the most judgmental—though they may hate a particular life genre they place themselves in that field of vision and sit there in a state of disgust as they engulf themselves in a mindset of hate. They look for reason to be mad and people to be mad at. They are the ones who drive down the road yelling at anyone who drives their car in a manner that they do not feel is appropriate. They are the ones who look for fights. And, the list goes on.

Though there are certainly all kinds of developmental and psychologically based reasons why each of us does anything that we do, the ultimate truth of life is, we are the <u>one</u> who has the potential to create who and what we ultimately are and who and what we ultimately become based upon what we choose to do. Thus, how you behave in life, what you say and what you do, is ultimately your choice. But, do you have the mental control to choose to remove yourself from the mentally addicting mindset of adrenalin filled hatred and accept a world of peace? Do you have the mental control to turn off your judgments and your interpersonal beliefs and allow each person to exist in their own state of perfection?

Emotions are what drives most of our lives. But, if we allow negative emotions to cause us to do what we do, then what does our life become? It becomes a selfish landscape driven by desire and the desire for other things and other people to be something that they are not.

Free yourself of hate. Free yourself of judgment. Let yourself embrace the peace and everything becomes better—maybe not as emotionally adrenalized, but better.

Do You Own the Copyright?
11/Jul/2017 07:58 AM

It's kind of funny... I was driving past this building today that used to house this business that I went to all of the time back in the mid 1990s. It was a place called Kinko's and they were one of the first business chains to offer easy self-access to color copy and printing options plus, for those people who did not own one, (and many people didn't back then), you could rent a computer in their computer room by the hour. As they were open twenty-four hours a day, I used to go there in the late night to make Production Packages and PR Kits for my movies and/or me.

Anyway, at some point in time the company became very aware of copyright law. So, anything that was being copied by them you had to show proof that you were the legal copyright holder.

Today, nobody gives two shits about the legality of copyright law and they, in fact, attempt to find all kinds of reasons and justifications to skirt this law. I say this all the time, but if you didn't envision it, if you didn't create it, if you didn't pay for its creation, you should have the self-respect not to use it for any other purpose than it was intended unless you receive permission from the owner. But, I am sure that point of law (and moral decency) falls to deaf ears so back to the point...

Anyway, I would go in there and hand them a poster for one of my films or a magazine cover I was on or something like that... In some cases, they would ask, *"Are you the copyright holder?"* My answer was, *"That's me!"*

Now, by this point of my life I was in my mid-thirties and to have a very young graveyard shifter giving me grief when I was giving them business really sent me in the wrong direction. In some cases, the people who worked there came to know me as the, *"B-movie guy,"* and I would have no problem. In other cases, some overzealous staff member would give me serious shit. *"Do you own the copyright?" "That's me!" "Well, what about company name on the bottom with the copyright tag?" "I own that company!" "Can you prove it?" "Where's your manager?" "We have no manager at night."* Sometimes they would just not copy my stuff and I would walk out of there substantially pissed. But, that's life. That's copyright law. Now, I can laugh about it. But, back then…

About a week ago I had an interesting copyright orientated situation occur. Someone from a printing house contacted one of the people that works with me and let them know someone had come into their shop with the intention of pressing a bunch of posters based on one of my films. They asked if we had designed the poster and/or had approved it. We did not. They did send us a copy of the poster and it was very well designed but it was not from us. This print shop did the right thing and turned the job down. But, I am sure the next print shop down the block was not be so vigilant, will take the job, and there will be a poster out there based on one of my films, created for what reason I don't know???

I think back further to a vaguely similar incident that took place a bit deeper in time. There was this one guy that I had given a part in one of my early Zen Films, *Samurai Vampire Bikers from Hell.* Though the guy was a supporting character he decided he wanted to have a poster made in association with the film with him as the central focus. Now, keep in mind, this was at a point in time when you didn't just make your poster(s) on your Mac at home or in your office. You had to take it to a big production house where it cost big bank to get them produced. But, the guy contacted me so he could go to my photographer, pay him, get the shot of himself that he needed, and then get the poster designed by a professional and created. The funny thing was, he never asked me if this was okay. He just did it. Anyway, he paid a lot of money to get a poster of himself, based on my film, created. Why? I have no idea. But, as it didn't damage anything, (no harm no foul), I just looked the other way.

You know, life is a funny thing... We all create. Some build houses, some stock shelves, some run numbers, some paint paintings, some make babies... Some people will love what you create while others will find a reason to hate you for what you create. Some of us create things that other people want to profit from; either financially or in other more non-descript ways. Though there are a lot of ways to come at it, I can only feel that there needs to be that space of respect given to the creations of others; somewhere between where Kinko's would not let me make copies of my own movie posters and the place where people just steal the creations of others, for whatever reason and motivation that they find it necessary to do that.

Somewhere, if you find it within yourself to create, that is the place where you have actually given back, given to the great whole and the greater good and actually done something. I think that is the best space to focus upon. Make your own creations don't find a reason to focus your life upon the creations of others.

The Problem with Being Fourteen
10/Jul/2017 03:19 PM

There is a problem when you are fourteen years ago. You have begun to feel like an adult but you have no true sense of what it takes to actually be an adult. Most likely, you are still living under the roof that your parents are paying for, you are getting money from your parents to buy your clothes and your objects of desire, yet you feel you have a voice and an opinion worth hearing. You make all kinds of statements about all of things that you will do. But, they are all off somewhere in the distance. Something you will do someday.

Some people never mentally grow past the age of fourteen. They are locked in the mindset of they are something, yet they do nothing. They scream their ideas and opinions to the world via the internet but they do nothing to make the world a better place or bring their dreams into reality. They just talk...

The fact is, opinions hurt an individual's life more than they help it. Why? Because they are not necessarily based in fact. They are based in personal speculation. Thus, though they may make a person act and/or feel a certain way, they do not contribute to the greater truth of reality. In fact, opinions, (whether based in truth or fiction), make people say and do all kinds of crazy things. In the long run of one's life, many of these things may come to define a person and do so in a very negative manner. Thus, the fourteen-year-old is never allowed to mature.

How many people do you know that are actually paying the bills and raising a family that have the time to become lost in youthful verbal masturbation? …Talking of what they think, what they will do someday, whom they love and whom they hate? What you will find is that they are too busy making a living so that their fourteen-year-old child can relax in that luxury, at least for a little while.

Even when you are young, you need to chart your life. Instead of talking, (and becoming lost in what your think and why you think it), you need to begin doing. For doing, is the essence of living a productive life.

If you are old and still locked in the mindset of the fourteen-year-old you once were, you need to wake up. What is what you are saying, based upon what you are thinking, motivated by who knows what, actually equaling in your life and the lives of all those you know? You need to stop being a fourteen-year-old, take responsibility, stop being lost in what you think, and go out there and contribute to life.

THE ZEN

www.ingramcontent.com/pod-product-compliance
Lightning Source LLC
Chambersburg PA
CBHW060414170426
43199CB00013B/2134